THE ENTREPRENEUR'S GUIDE TO RAISING CAPITAL FROM ANGEL INVESTORS

THE ENTREPRENEUR'S GUIDE TO RAISING CAPITAL FROM ANGEL INVESTORS

TARBY BRYANT
FOUNDER OF
THE GATHERING OF ANGELS

Published by Deeds Publishing
Marietta, GA
www.deedspublishing.com

Library of Congress Cataloging-in-Publications Data is available upon request.

ISBN 978-1-941165-35-5

Books are available in quantity for promotional or premium use. For information, write Deeds Publishing, PO Box 682212, Marietta, GA 30068 or info@deedspublishing.com.

First Edition

10 9 8 7 6 5 4 3 2 1

CONTENTS

PREFACE

IN THE MID-1990S, I WAS SERVING AS A SENIOR CONSULTANT TO A non-profit corporation based in Albuquerque, New Mexico. Our organization was tasked with commercializing technologies coming out of the National Laboratories based in Los Alamos and Sandia. Both labs were developing ideas and devices in conjunction with their national mission that had the potential for commercial appeal—*if* the lab employees, called "principal investigators," could develop a business plan and find the needed seed and early stage capital.

Annual Venture Capital conferences were held in May in Albuquerque. Venture Capitalists (VCs) would fly in from around the country for several days of presentations, fine spicy New Mexican cuisine, and world class speakers. The lab rats (principal investigators) had been coached intensely; once they'd received venture capital funding, they would then move out of New Mexico and take up residence in the state where the VC firm was domiciled. The VCs wanted to closely monitor their investments, and the young companies literally *followed the money.* At that time, New Mexico had no Angel groups, no VC funds, no Investment Bankers, and no banks willing to support these laboratories.

Earlier, during the late 1970s, another young company, called Microsoft, started in Albuquerque with Bill Gates and Paul Allen as senior officers and founders. They came to the New Mexico city after reading an article in *Popular Mechanics* about a new device called the Altair computer that would challenge the typewriter—and might change our business world forever. While in New Mexico, the Microsoft team wrote a program for an operating system called DOS (Disk Operating System) and began to install it into the Altair computer. As the system began to work, Gates and Allen were advised to protect the intellectual property around DOS with a patent. They engaged a respected local law firm to assist in this process; once completed, the law firm submitted an itemized bill for $55,000 and expected timely payment. Neither Gates nor Allen had $55,000 and the local banks were only lending on cows, uranium, and gold bricks. Gates offered stock and warrants in his new company as payment, but the law firm respectfully declined, to their everlasting regret.

Therefore, with no VCs and no investment banks in New Mexico, Bill Gates did what every creative and resourceful entrepreneur would do: he called home to his Dad, a successful and wealthy attorney in Seattle. Gates Sr. offered to cover the legal bill on the condition that Bill, Paul Allen, and the software engineers and geeks leave Albuquerque and move back to Seattle where Mr. Gates Sr. could more closely oversee and monitor his investment. This loss of Microsoft to Seattle underscores the problem new companies face when they're left without sources of seed and early stage capital. So, Microsoft followed the money—making Microsoft millionaires in Washington State instead of New Mexico.

The stage was set in 1996. After surveying the capital landscape, a growing number of companies that started up in New Mexico went on to find capital out of state—and subsequently left the Land of Enchantment. I realized, with my background in Economic Development, that back in my home state of Georgia, that unless we stopped this outmigration of young companies, our state economy would enter a death spiral.

While reading my *Forbes* magazine late one night (no doubt with a glass of good red wine), I saw a very long article about a group in the Silicon Valley called The Band of Angels. Its leader, a man by the name of Dr. Hans Severans, had organized a group of wealthy accredited investors who would gather in Palo Alto one a month to dine and hear from three to four young companies seeking seed capital. As soon as I read about it, I thought—this was just what New Mexico needed! By good fortune, Dr. Severans was on a panel later that month at Los Alamos—so I attended and asked twenty or more questions. We became good friends and he offered to guide me in establishing a similar group in New Mexico. I thought we might call it the Santa Fe Band of Angels, but he would absolutely not hear of it!

The following week, I came up with my own name for our New Mexico version: I called us The Gathering of Angels and held my first meeting on a Saturday morning in mid-October 1996, at 8:30 am at Santa Fe's Eldorado Hotel. Because I was teaching Corporate Finance four nights a week all over New Mexico, I had no time for evening meetings—just for breakfast. We enjoyed the requisite black coffee, juice, muffins, and fresh fruit and had two to four presenting companies for three successive months. But…no capital funding occurred.

Confused, frustrated, and bewildered, I called Hans to try to figure out what I was doing wrong. He simply asked, "What kind of wine are you serving?" Well, none—in America we generally don't have wine with breakfast. That, apparently, was the problem. Hans explained to me that Angels do not write checks at breakfast; they only do so at night and only if they've had good wine. So I stopped teaching one night, changed my business model, and started having dinner meetings with wine—and the funding began rolling in.

380+ capital fundings later, I'm still doing what I love: helping young companies prepare for and receive needed seed and early stage capital.

The Gathering of Angels (GOA) continued in its efforts to assist New Mexico-based companies in finding capital until 2000, when we decided to spread the GOA process and practice to other cities across the USA. Starting in Atlanta, Georgia, we had meetings monthly in Carmel, Scottsdale, Dallas, Houston, Austin, Washington DC, Charlotte, Hilton Head, and Jacksonville. We changed with the times when the Great Recession arrived in late 2007 by pulling back and holding meetings only in Santa Fe and Atlanta.

The GOA Business Model is SEC approved and their lawyers have encouraged our efforts to help entrepreneurs access needed seed and early stage capital. Angels, VCs and Investment Bankers attend GOA meetings complimentary and normally write checks one to fifteen days after attending. This period allows for proper due diligence and second and third meetings with the management team, review of securities documents, and final decisions on amount of capital fundings. Each GOA selected presenter pays a fixed upfront fee with no % of capital fundings. The Gathering of Angels is not an Angel *club* but an Angel *forum,* where individuals write checks directly to an entrepreneurial company. The money is neither pooled nor aggregated, and individuals considering investment do their own due diligence and make their own investment decisions.

Based on the experience learned in my years with GOA, I decided it was time to capture that experience in this easy to use book. What you will read here will provide entrepreneurs with a guidepost as well as detailed and time tested approaches to raising seed and early stage capital from Accredited Angel Investors.

After you have exhausted your personal savings, cashed in all your 401k plans, tapped out your friends, close family, and relatives (who decline to return your pleading calls for money)—you are ready for Angel Investors. Angels normally invest $25,000 to $2,000,000 in capital—and because they take the risk of being very early investors: they expect and can demand a more than generous return on their capital.

This book will show you among other things how to prepare for an Angel meeting, what documents to bring, how to dress, what to say and—perhaps just as importantly—what *not* to say. We will discuss in detail the concept that I call "The Art of the Deal"—something that involves valuing an often pre-revenue company and pricing of stock in the new venture capital raise. You will learn my preferred valuation methodology using discounted cash flow with a 40% IRR. You will see how to develop a strong but ever flexible 20-35 page business plan, a tight one to two page executive summary, and a realistic and defensible three to five year P&L projection. We will cover the importance of assembling a strong management team, board of advisors, and board of directors when you have no capital to pay for this needed talent.

The content of this book will teach what has worked in raising capital, what to avoid doing or saying when presenting, how critical preparation is, and how to close the deal and get a check from an Angel Investor. Even if you are a seasoned entrepreneur who has raised millions, the capital landscape *does* change and there are always new tricks to learn and implement for your next venture. New offerings like the Invest Georgia Exemption open up new channels for capital from unaccredited Investors who want to venture into these turbulent waters.

This book is not a fast read to dismiss to your library bookshelf upon completing. It is a "how to" guide full of material for underlining and highlighting—one to which you can return when different sections are needed to address a new challenge. I provide advice and suggestions from my eighteen years of operating The Gathering of Angels across the USA throughout the book. But more importantly, you'll hear from current and past Angel Investors and Entrepreneurs alike who are in the trenches daily, raising capital and investing in young companies. Successful seed capital investing is not proper British warfare but hand to hand jungle combat with high risks and potentially high rewards for the smart Angel Investor with exceptional timing and focused attention, who seeks opportunities where markets, recessionary cycles, and the FED current policies cooperate.

I am thankful for my loving family and good friends who granted me the time to write this book. They seem to understand the importance of this project, not just to me as its author but to Entrepreneurs worldwide. All of these individuals need to understand better the Angel capital process and how to prepare for their chance to grab the "Gold Ring" of Angel capital.

I hope I have provided you with an enjoyable, worthwhile and informative reading experience. May this book always be close at hand as your definitive reference guide for finding capital from Angel Investors.

Tarby Bryant
Big Canoe, Georgia
Summer 2014

1. ENTREPRENEURIAL SURVIVAL SKILLS

IF YOU ENJOY A STRICT NINE-TO-FIVE WEEKDAY WORK SCHEDULE AND free time on the weekends to spend as you please, then the life of a 21ˢᵗ century Entrepreneur may not be a fit for you. If you enjoy quiet evenings at home after work and leaving the cares of the day at your work place, you may want to reconsider heading out on your own. If that regular paycheck and monthly contributions into your 401k plan are necessary, you may want to consider just reading about the life of an Entrepreneur, instead of becoming one.

After college, most young folks are just looking for a steady paycheck to pay bills, leave the family home, get an apartment or small house, and start a family. Most of these financial requirements suggest a "real job"; they don't lead to the path of Entrepreneur embraced by individuals like Bill Gates, Paul Allen, Mark Zuckerberg, Mark Cuban, and countless others. Most entrepreneurs nowadays will work for some period of time in a safe, friendly environment with a steady paycheck and then jump out of the boat into uncharted waters.

Growing up in a family business in Atlanta, I had the best of both worlds. My Dad was an entrepreneur who started our family business in the Automobile Club industry and grew it to a $3M enterprise that operated in nine southeastern states. I caught the start-up disease at a young age, with my earliest entrepreneurial venture in the fireworks business: I would buy fireworks in South Carolina and bring them back for sale in the Atlanta area. This venture came to an end, however, when my hidden stash exploded and my hooch in the deep woods went up in smoke. After the fire department was called in to extinguish the four alarm blaze that threatened the burn down nearby East Rivers Elementary School, my first business venture had to close its doors.

But it wouldn't be my last. My next memorable venture was selling red-hot balls on the playground of little Lovett School. But that ended when the Principal caught me red handed with the goods—selling candy on school property wasn't allowed. I also ran a movie theatre from my home's basement, but not all of my movie customers were happy with the fact that I priced my hot dogs at $1 apiece. Some of my close friends and former neighbors even remind me of that to this day

Much later, in the 1960s, I was fresh out of Vietnam, ready to apply the MBA in Finance, with honors, that I had earned prior to my Vietnam adventure. I started my first real venture as a subsidiary of the motor club in the car rental and leasing business. My Dad and I signed the notes at the bank and suddenly, I was the CEO of Bryant Auto Rental and Leasing. I hired staff and opened locations around Atlanta; we competed with Hertz, Avis, National, and Budget and came in a distant fifth place. This venture survived three years and closed when the local banks, our main source of capital, decided they would get into the auto leasing business and squeezed us out.

I did go on to enter the real estate brokerage and land syndication and later hotel development and acquisition businesses with much better success than my first ventures. I had the entrepreneurial disease, and in 1985 left the family auto club business to strike out on my own in the hospitality business. At one point, I had eight hotel ventures going, ranging from a 19 room bed & breakfast in Savannah called the Ballastone Inn to a 500 room Hyatt Regency in Nashville. Today, my crown jewel is the 221 room, 53 stories Four Seasons Hotel on 14th Street in mid-town Atlanta.

This was all thrilling to me; but the life of an Entrepreneur is not for the faint in heart. You must decide really who you are; those who are married must proceed not only with their spouse's consent but their full blessing. You must know what kind of life you enjoy and want to live going forward. These survival skills, as I call them, are either ingrained in your DNA from birth, as they were with me, or become acquired skills and behavioral patterns. We find these traits and tendencies in most successful Entrepreneurs. Of course, we all are different, live in different parts of the country or world, and are exposed to different environmental influences. These distinctions enhance the journey; but it's undeniable that we can recognize certain patterns that lead to success.

Entrepreneurs must be *healthy, fit,* and *have high energy.* Physical attributes allow them to push beyond the usual 9 to 5 hours. The life of an entrepreneur starts early and often ends late; you are on the go 24-7, 365. Your day may begin at the O-K Café at 7AM and end at 9PM after drinks and dinner at Chops in Buckhead. Couch potatoes need not apply for this entrepreneurial lifestyle.

An entrepreneur must be *focused*. Having a passion for three different ventures in three completely different industries will not cut it as all of your energy, attention, and absolute focus need to be on a single endeavor's success. I often meet young entrepreneurs at the Gathering of Angels looking for seed capital for three companies they're looking to launch—and are seeking funding for all three, or any one of the above. It's a huge challenge to start a business from ground zero; if your attention and concentration is diffused and unfocused, you don't stand a chance. One new exciting undertaking at a time is enough, especially given your other responsibilities in life and family.

Survival skills like *creativity* are critical. Most in-demand products and services are out there already. In order to effectively compete, you will need a high level of ingenuity to uncover a niche where you can offer something that customers don't have yet. Copying what four others already have in the marketplace is sure to lead to failure. Your competitors often have more money and channels of distribution. You will get killed unless your offering is so novel that it's able to attract market acceptance.

Another requisite survival skill is *adaptability*. The unmet needs you discover today will likely be filled with competitors tomorrow. You'll face lots of challenges, and will need to be flexible and willing to adjust and make course changes as necessary. Plans B and C are the order of the day for an entrepreneur's mostly uncharted course map. Every day when the sun rises, his path is new and fresh with ever-evolving opportunities. Rigid plans and closed minds do not fit here. I don't discourage making plans, but they should not be cast in stone and bound in a leather binder. They will most assuredly change monthly, weekly, often daily—sometimes even hourly. If you are flexible, resilient, and open to the excitement of new challenges every day, you may fit the model of an Entrepreneur.

Entrepreneurs must also be *coachable* and never so arrogant that they forget to heed the wisdom of other's advice and suggestions. Advice will come at you in all manners and forms, you need to consider and value what others with more experience are telling you. I frequently encounter presenters at my Gathering of Angels meetings who think they have all the answers; they're prepared their PowerPoint presentation and are not open to our advice and suggestions for improving it. One even claimed that, "I have been doing these presentations for a living for the last 20 years; I do not need practice and your suggestions." Needless to say, he left the GOA stage and monthly event with no money.

An Entrepreneur must be willing to *relocate* to where they can find a source of capital. You may enjoy living in the small town in Kentucky where your family has lived for three centuries; but if your capital source is in Atlanta, Boston, Silicon Valley, or Dallas, well...that's where you'll be heading. Venture Capitalists often demand that a young firm move to where they are located to better and more closely monitor their forward progress. Additionally, these major cities often have better infrastructure and larger talent pools for employees.

Finally, Entrepreneurs must be able to communicate their vision clearly. If you are shy and tend to avoid sharing your view and opinions of meaningful things, the life of an Entrepreneur may not be for you. You must have a good command of the English language, along with writing and speaking skills to convey your company story both inside to your team and to the outside world. Speak Up, Toastmasters, and Dale Carnegie programs can be helpful if you are lacking in the skill set and are coachable.

Entrepreneurs are constantly on a roller coaster ride filled with high drama and bursts of jubilation, with many moments of despair and discouragement. That big contract you were counting on has fallen apart; your Chief Technology Officer got a better job offer that you can't match; the bank called and your account is overdrawn; ABCs check bounced; the IRS wants a visit with you and your CFO; and the list goes on. If you want excitement, unbridled joy, and heart wrenching defeat, join the ranks of Entrepreneurs worldwide who would never return to corporate life. Check your personal tool box before you head out on this journey called Entrepreneurship. Again—it is definitely not for the faint of heart.

ANGEL INVESTOR OBSERVATIONS AND COMMENTS

1. I like a steady paycheck, but I dream of being an entrepreneur.
2. I know the banking business cold; maybe I will start my own restaurant.
3. After 10 years working for The Man, I am ready to be my own boss.
4. I had this dream about a new widget for the kitchen.

5. I have ten crazy ideas per week; one of them will surely make me rich.
6. Working for a startup is too risky; they could go under.
7. After 30 years at IBM, I am ready to open my new wine venture.
8. I enjoy a regular paycheck and always will….not for me.
9. I want to invest in an entrepreneur that is focused and 100% committed to this venture.
10. The CEO is doing six things and none of them well. He's all over the place; I am out!
11. The CEO is not adaptable to change and will get killed in the jungle.
12. The Presenter at GOA was horrible and needs public speaking lessons.
13. The CEO could not answer the three questions asked in a responsible manner.

REFLECTIVE QUESTIONS FOR CHAPTER 1

1. What are five characteristics of an Entrepreneur?

_____
_____
_____
_____
_____

2. Where can I learn how to be an Entrepreneur and survive in the jungle?

_____
_____
_____

3. I have a Ph.D. in Nuclear Physics; does that make me an Entrepreneur?

_____
_____
_____

4. I am a bit set in my ways and inflexible, will those traits make me a good and successful Entrepreneur?

    _____

    _____

    _____

5. I enjoy and require a steady paycheck. Can I make it as an Entrepreneur?

    _____

    _____

    _____

2. WHAT IS AN ANGEL INVESTOR?

THIS CHAPTER'S TITLE IS ONE OF THE MANY QUESTIONS THAT KEEP ENTRE-preneurs up at night. Their internal monologue goes something like:

How can I meet one? How can I get him/her to invest in my start-up and tap into their network for new distribution channels, capital, and corporate relations? I've exhausted my savings, tapped out my 401k plans, and even worn out Uncle Willie, who has loaned me money in the past for my failed crazy ventures, is not returning my insistent calls. My parents love me but cannot assist with any more funding—I need fresh capital to grow my business. I have called Donald Trump, Warren Buffett, and Mark Zuckerberg to no avail. I have visited my local bank but, to my surprise and absolute amazement, they are making business loans only on established businesses with a three-year track record of profitable operations, audited financial statements, fully developed management teams, personal guarantees, and real collateral (whatever that is). I am probably too early stage for Venture Capital and Investment Bankers but I know they will be knocking on my door later. Am I just dreaming? Can I really make this business a reality?

My current management team for this venture is committed emotionally, perform work as needed, but have no capital resources to invest in my new company. They're living from paycheck to paycheck and collectively could not invest $50K in my new dream company but are working now for stock at night and have a full time paying gig elsewhere to support their families. I have very few contacts with money. I grew up in a middle class family in the South; though I graduated from a good state college it certainly wasn't Harvard, Yale, Wharton, or Stanford—so I don't have the imbedded network that comes from attending such institutions. Most of my classmates found entry-level jobs after graduation; none opted to be Entrepreneurs like *me. I have heard about Angel Investors but have not recognized any guys with pin striped suites and angel wings tucked under their jackets or sweaters at Starbucks, Subway, or my local Chamber networking functions recently.*

Angel Investors have been around a long time; however, they've only been moderately visible and recognized as a real and viable source of capital for young entrepreneurial companies in the last 25 years. The concept started with the funding of movies in Hollywood and new shows on Broadway. A producer or director would craft a movie or play, begin hiring the cast and getting the set ready—and realize very quickly his or her resources were insufficient to fund the venture and that he'd need huge amounts of capital to pull off the next blockbuster. Banks in those days would sometimes provide partial funding, but hard equity was needed. At that time, Investment Bankers and VCs were not interested in movies or plays and the producers were on a mad search for equity capital. Many wealthy individuals lived in New York or Los Angeles / Hollywood and often made investments in risky ventures. Movies and plays fit that model and could potentially provide eight to ten times return on their investment, if successful. With more losers than winners, movies and plays provided a chance to invest now, pray you picked a winner, and hope for a huge return on capital invested.

The trend caught on. During the late 70s and early 80s, California's Silicon Valley began to develop as a hotbed of technology companies. Surrounded by world class educational institutions like Stanford, it became the epicenter of early Angel Investing. Wealthy residents would roll the dice on young start-ups by putting in $10,000 to $1 million dollars in hopes of a 10X return on capital. Entrepreneurs inhabited coffee houses and bars, and Angels would circle them looking for the next Microsoft or Apple. Chance meetings and introductions by legal and accounting professionals produced needed capital for Silicon Valley young start-ups.

In the late 80s, these Angel Investors would start clubs and gatherings where young companies would come and make presentations over dinner and wine. The grandfather of all angel clubs was the Silicon Valley based "Band of Angels" introduced in this book's Preface, founded by Dr. Hans Severans. Hans started hosting dinners at private clubs in the area, where he invites wealthy Californians to come and join him for an evening filled with investment opportunities, good food, and lots of wine. The attendees would review two to four young companies seeking seed and early stage capital; they'd then vet these companies, then select to present to a dinner meeting of 20-40 wealthy accredited Angel Investors. As the gate keeper and host of the meeting, Hans had Angel Investors lining up to attend and either jointly or individually making high risk investments in these start-ups. The Silicon Valley was flush with capital and highly paid executives who were anxious to find lucrative investment opportunities. The Band of Angels' monthly meetings delivered this opportunity.

The Angel clubs and gatherings provided an assured highly social opportunity, a chance to see early stage investment opportunities, and the ability to draw on the expertise and wisdom of others in the specific area of the company's focus and direction. Industry knowledge, distribution channels, skilled management expertise, and wise counsel in case of train wrecks was then and today important contributions that Angel Investors uniquely offer a young company in addition to seed capital. With a strong leader in Dr. Hans Severans, the Band of Angels made many wise and highly profitable investments. They backed a few losers but, on balance, produced a high return on invested angel capital. The Band of Angels also attracted substantial press and developed a waiting list of local Angel Investors who wanted to get on board this fast moving investment train. With large crowds of investors, young start-up companies lined up as well to present and get on the Dance Card for future events.

I lived in Santa Fe in the mid-90s, after taking an assignment with a non-profit venture called Technology Venture Corporation (TVC) out of Albuquerque. The organization was a subsidiary of Lockheed Martin, tasked with the responsibility of managing Sandia National Laboratory. We had a consulting contract with Los Alamos National Labs as well. I was responsible for the outreach to Los Alamos and would visit the Lab weekly to assist with commercialization of Lab-related technologies— helping the "Lab Rats" develop business plans, marketing plans, valuation, and financial structures to raise capital.

TVC also hosted an annual Equity Capital symposium. 15-20 young companies would come to the two day event and make 15 minute presentations to an assembled audience of 100-125 folks from around the country. Angel Investors, Venture Capitalists, and Investment Bankers would pay to attend this event for the exposure to young NM companies. As a member of the team that hosted this event for two years, I saw firsthand how this process helped secure funding for the New Mexico companies. However, I also observed that once they were funded, the

New Mexico company often went to where the money was and left the state. As I described in this book's Preface, the company got the capital they needed—but the State of New Mexico lost the employment and expertise.

You'll also remember from the Preface that Bill Gates and Paul Allen started Microsoft in Albuquerque back in the 1970s, but left because they could not raise seed capital in New Mexico to pay a $55,000 legal bill. When I read the *Forbes Magazine* story on the Silicon Valley based Band of Angels and Dr. Hans Severans, light bulbs went off in my head. What if we could start a Band of Angels in Santa Fe and replicate what Hans had done in the Silicon Valley? Though New Mexico was not quite the hotbed of technology, we *did* have three National Laboratories—and all the potential spin-off commercialization.

So where can you as an entrepreneur looking for seed and early stage capital find your Angel Investor—or even better, *several* of them to fuel your planned growth and capital needs? Where can you find people with money who are liquid and will listen to your pitch? You'll rarely find them in Gravel Switch, Kentucky, or Commerce, Georgia, or other small towns. You might locate some in resort communities like Santa Fe, New Mexico; Sea Island, Georgia; Jackson Hole, Wyoming; Pinehurst, North Carolina; or Pebble Beach, California. But most of the time, they are in big cities where they made their money. They may have cashed out and retired, or they might still be working because they enjoy the hunt.

You won't often come across Angels on the front page of the local paper. More often than not, they're behind the scenes investors and a meaningful force in the maturation process of young companies. You might find them on the golf course or in private clubs or fine dining facilities. They frequent the finer hotels in larger cities and more than likely fly first class or on a private jet. They may frequent McDonalds for a coffee or latte but you will rarely find them in the corner table. Angels value, honor, and respect the introductions and referrals they get from their respected lawyers and CPAs. Angels come in all shapes and sizes; but they're always hidden. They never wear a sign or name tag identifying them as an Angel Investor.

Each Angel Investor has a different perspective on investing, and need to be treated as such. They each made their capital in a novel and unique way. Some may have taken the old fashion approach—inherited it from family, parents, or relatives. Most made it from their company when it sold, or their employer when they retired or cashed out. Some have made wise and timely investments and then sold out; often they reinvest and do it again and again. Some Angel Investors only invest in familiar space where they have understanding, contacts for vetting, and genuine passion.

Other Angels have told me they only invest in the automotive industry, since that is all they know—then after forty years at Ford, they'll surprise me and put $400K into a B&B in the mountains of Colorado. Some angels want to invest solo; others need the security and joint due diligence of a group investment or Angel Clubs. Most Angel Investors, though, make their decisions and rely on "gut feel" and emotions over detailed research. VCs and Investment Bankers undergo a more thorough decision process; they'll usually take one to six months mulling things over and will often pass on projects if their discomfort level increases and risks and fear factors come to light.

In my view, Angel Investors offer more to a start-up than any other source of capital that you might attract to your venture. With your own savings and capital, you lack the wise advice and sound counsel of a seasoned warrior at your side. With capital from friends and family who love you deeply, you might attract money, but rarely industry knowledge, guidance for the road ahead, and assistance in quality introductions. The Venture Capital that might come later in your growth process could attract capital and sometimes a helpful senior partner—but you are often assigned a newly-minted MBA associate who has not been to many rodeos.

A true Angel Investor can often provide the needed seed and early stage capital but also industry expertise, contacts and introductions, and sage advice. As a start-up Entrepreneur, you are best served at this stage by an Angel Investor in your company's growth. You mission now is to find him/her and bring them on board as part of your team—not just an absentee financial partner in your journey.

Why would a wealthy Angel Investor write you a check for $20,000 to $1 million? Let's assume that you secure an audience, meet over lunch, dinner or coffee in private. Now your job is to very quickly, cogently, in 20-30 minutes convince him to invest his precious capital and his time in your start-up.

Are you prepared? Do you have your SEC documents in order, prepared by a securities attorney? Do you have your very tight one page Executive Summary and 20-slide PowerPoint vetted and ready at a moment's notice? Do you know your pre-money valuation? Do you know how your investors will get their money back (called a liquidity event or exit strategy)? Have you assembled your management team and advisors? Are you ready for input and sage advice from an Angel Investor and not just a passive family member?

You only get one chance to make the right impression in how you dress, act, and speak, and most certainly in raising seed and early stage capital. Kissing lots of frogs looking for your Prince or Princess is time consuming—and proper preparation can most assuredly shorten the process from your first date to consummation and check writing. This short but instructive primer will guide you through the process of raising capital—and how you can be better prepared and armed when your time comes for a face-to-face with an Angel Investor.

REAL ANGEL INVESTOR OBSERVATIONS AND COMMENTS

1. I have made my money, sold my business, and I'm now looking for some excitement in retirement. Golf is getting boring.
2. I have cashed out and have $500K to invest in 7-10 young companies. I hope to make it big in one or two.
3. Angel investing is risky, but I can afford it and enjoy the ride.
4. Angel Investing requires faith and patience; time will tell if I made the right decision.
5. I want to put money in but also want to assist and counsel management. That will help improve their chances of survival and ultimate success.
6. Valuations must be realistic for me, as an early investor, to not take a big haircut with the next round of financing.
7. CEO projections are never correct and always inflated. I always discount them by 50-75% or more.
8. A company's capital seeking offerings must be investor attractive and give me 40-50% IRR in exchange for my taking this early risk.
9. Will my early investment in combination with other investors be enough to get the young company off the runway?

10. To get my investment interest, the market addressed must be large, with high margins, and limited competition.

11. I like the concept and market size, but the management team is weak and unseasoned.

12. I enjoy angel investing and have cashed out of two deals, have three walking wounded, and buried three others. This ride is not for the faint of heart.

13. I have invested in three deals in the last few years but rarely hear from the CEOs of my young companies. They have forgotten me.

14. I like the concept and marketing plan; but the CEO is arrogant and does not listen well.

15. My first question is, "What is your unfair competitive advantage" over the other three or four companies doing the same thing in this space? And don't tell me there are no competitors and you will be first to market.

16. If you want my investment dollars, your books and records must be current and up to date.

17. I do not make grants; I look for a risk related return on my investment made in your company. Paying me a 5% ROI is not accounting for the risk. Go see your banker at Wells Fargo or Chase.

18. I want my investment capital back in two to three years; I may not be around in ten years as you propose in your presentation.

19. Call me again when you finish your business plan.

REFLECTIVE QUESTIONS FOR CHAPTER 2

1. What is an Angel Investor?

_____

_____

_____

2. Where do Angel Investors nest?

_____

_____

_____

3. When are Angel Investors important to your new venture?

    _____

    _____

    _____

4. How are you Uncle George and an Angel Investor different?

    _____

    _____

    _____

5. What do Angel Investors look for in an early stage investment?

    _____

    _____

    _____

3. THE BUSINESS PLAN

THE FIRST AND MOST IMPORTANT STEP IN STARTING A NEW BUSINESS VEN-
ture, or buying one for repositioning and growth, is to create a 25-35
page document called a Business Plan. If you are not committed to developing such a plan, you are probably not ready to be an Entrepreneur
and might consider remaining in your current job. Let me be very clear:
you must complete the business plan; you cannot hire someone else to
create it. Often professionals or grant writers will suggest they can do
the plan for you and charge you $1,000 to $10,000—and occasionally
even (falsely) guarantee that you will raise money from their plan. The
fact that it is *their plan* is exactly the problem; it does not come from *your*
heart and brain.

Though it's a time consuming process, completing the plan gives
you a road map and compass to get customers, hire management team
members, and attract seed and early stage capital. Without a business
plan, you are dead in the water. The first question I asked when an
Entrepreneur calls me looking for capital is: can I read your business
plan and tight executive summary. People will often reply by telling me
that I just need to listen to his pitch or see this or that video and trust
me, this is a huge market and my widget will be well received with no real
competition. When I press for delivery of their business plan, it usually
becomes clear that their "plan" is entirely in their head.

No new venture will raise capital from Angel Investors like me
without a well-crafted business plan. It is the first thing we ask for,
and we study it with high due diligence. Venture Capitalists will often
re-write your plan and readjust your projections; they'll most certainly
chop your valuation before they issue a Term Sheet with their offer
to invest in your company. The Business Plan is an ever evolving
document; it's not something you bind in a hard leather jacket and put
on the shelf. Instead, you should keep this valuable document handy for

reference, constant revision, and modification. Business today is ever changing; the acceleration of technology has made it such that you're able to alter your Business Plan as new products or offerings appear in the competitive landscape, new management talent is attracted to your venture, and economic and financial pressures influence your business, I can promise that once you've created it, this document will change before you have finished the last sections of writing. Nothing in business stays the same for long—and your Business Plan has to mirror this fluidity. Thus, an easily updated electronic copy of your Business Plan is critical—available to print or forward electronically to those who want to review it.

By now you're likely wondering: where do you go to get guidance and direction on how to produce a quality Business Plan? Can I go to the Internet or the cloud for guidance, or is there software on a CD for a template? The answer to all of these is "yes." There are numerous delivery platforms available that cost from $75 to $200—most assuredly, money well spent. Each offering will provide you a tailored, industry-specific format for your Business Plan. They help reduce the odds that you'll miss critical elements Angel Investors expect when they inspect your finished product. *Biz Plan Builder* by JIAN and *Biz Plan Pro* by Palo Alto software are my recommended choices; both are available online or in Office Depot or Staples. These two industry leaders for the creation of your Business Plan now offer cloud based SAS delivery formats. While there are numerous books and texts that also offer formats and chapter headings, these provide an easy to follow menu of topics you need to cover, as well as guidance and resources for completion.

Once you have made the commitment to get started, bought the software, and installed it on your laptop, you are ready to begin creating your Business Plan. As your journey begins, you will want keep your work papers, projections, and all documents involved in the process in a file folder or on your hard drive for easy repeated reference. It takes a great deal of discipline and commitment to complete the plan. But, rest assured, this tenacity will be rewarded when you meet your Angel Investor and can say, "Yes Sir, here is my plan and I am prepared and excited to walk you through all aspects of my new business venture." A very tight Executive Summary—included in the first one to three pages— is the first thing an Angel Investor will read. If it sufficiently interests and intrigues them, they will then request your full Business Plan.

The essential parts of a well-crafted Business Plan are:

1. The one-to-three page Executive Summary;
2. One to five pages on the product or service offered;
3. The market analysis;
4. Discussion of competition and how your product or service is better that competition;
5. Clarification of distribution channels;
6. Information on your management team, advisors, and board of directors;
7. One-, three-, and five-year profit and loss projections in some detail;
8. Snapshot financial summaries and margins;
9. Capital sought in this first round;
10. Use of funds;
11. Exit strategies for early investors.

You need to address capital and corporate structure in the plan, and cite reasons for the location you've chosen for your business. Think of the Business Plan as a sales document; it needs to have *sizzle*. If it's not positive and forward looking, you will not attract capital to your new venture. It's a good idea once you finish your business plan to circulate it to your management team, advisors, and board members for their review and honored critique before you go out to meet with your first Angel Investor. Have a CPA or seasoned MBA review your financial projections and valuation methodologies. The more constructive input and modifications to your plan, the stronger and more defensible it will be to the forthcoming barrage of questions and comments from Angel Investors—like the following.

REAL ANGEL INVESTOR OBSERVATIONS AND COMMENTS

1. Without a full developed business plan, I would never consider investing in your venture.
2. Two pages of marketing materials do not constitute a Business Plan.
3. Your PowerPoint Presentation was strong—but where is your business plan?
4. I need to understand where you are heading.

5. Good Business Plan—but, you completely left out information on your management team.
6. You had fifteen spelling errors in the first ten pages. Did you read this over or even use spell check?
7. Did Merlyn the Magician do your financial projections—or some other wizard?
8. Your Business Plan needs to be formatted.
9. Your plan makes no mention of competition—yet my Google research suggests 10-12 big players in this space.
10. You have mixed up P&L statements with Balance Sheet items. Who reviewed these projections?
11. You are clearly a marketing guy; you need to hire someone to help you with the financial side and capital needs.

REFLECTIVE QUESTIONS FOR CHAPTER 3

1. Why do I need to write a Business Plan?

    _____
    _____
    _____

2. Where can I find help and assistance in the creation of my Business Plan?

    _____
    _____
    _____

3. What are the seven basic parts of a well-drafted Business Plan?

    _____
    _____
    _____

4. Is a Business Plan a "cast in stone" document?

    _____
    _____
    _____

5. Why should I not hire someone else to write my Business Plan?

_____

_____

_____

4. CAPITAL, THE ROCKET FUEL OF THE ENTREPRENEURIAL COMPANY

WITH YOUR COMPLETE BUSINESS PLAN COMPLETED AND SAFELY HOUSED in both your three-ring binder and on your hard drive, you have discovered that your company will quickly outgrow your savings and 401k plan from your last real employer. Your plan has allowed you to quickly recognize that you'll need $500,000 within the first 12 months to launch your rocket ship and sustain it till orders and cash flow exceed current expenses and immediate capital needs. Breaking even is a wonderful experience, but in order to get there, you need that initial funding. Now is the time to begin exploring all sources, and calculate how much of your new venture you will have to give up, how many convertible notes will be signed, and if there are grants possible. You must look into the latter because this is free capital that you don't have to repay—and none of your stock is issued for this needed infusion.

Your savings are exhausted and your team members have little capital to contribute. Your family that loves you deeply is very concerned that you resigned from the steady paycheck job that supported your family for the last ten years after college and graduate school. Your parents are now in retirement and hoping that you, your wife, and your two kids won't need to move back in with them. You do have some wealthy friends who've made short term loans to your new venture, but soon you'll need to pay these back and start a search for real equity Angel Investors. Your visits to the local banks have not proven fruitful as your new venture does not have a track record of three profitable years or audited statements and your personal collateral is limited and certainly not liquid. Your visits to the local SBDC and SBA offices were enlightening and informative but their 7A program does not fit your high tech venture. You have heard about Angel Investors and read much about Venture Capital; now you need to start your capital campaign in earnest before you run out of rocket fuel.

Chapter 2 of this book clarified what an Angel Investor is, where they hang out, and what they look for in a potential new venture investment. Your task now is to take your new Business Plan and the capital needs of $500,000 you have for the next 12 months and properly package an appealing offering. Then, get cleaned up, pull out your sport jacket and tie—and prepare for battle. You can't prepare for this capital adventure overnight; it requires much thought, and good legal and accounting advice. Your retired ambulance chasing personal injury attorney uncle is not a good choice for someone to draft your securities documents to meet SEC standards. You must certainly do the 1-3-5 year P&L projections yourself—but a CPA's quick review will bring reality and accuracy to these projections and forward looking statements. Input from your team on the business plan has gotten them involved; they might have leads to Angel Investors and sources of capital in their circle of friends. Building a hot list of prospects is critical at this point. You'll need to make a lot of connections before you find someone to write you and your venture that investment check.

Now you must start your research into Angel Clubs and Angel Forums across the country and in most big metro cities. The Gathering of Angels is just one of many Angel Forums that allow entrepreneurial companies to come across the country or from the local area to make presentations seeking capital. Each club or forum is distinct; each one has different requirements and often geographic restrictions. For example, the Band of Angels only considers Silicon Valley companies. Other groups only deal with technology and some specialize in funding software ventures. Your research and due diligence will need to be focused and committed to get the results you need: an audience and chance to present your new venture for this capital round. Checking the different Angel groups' references, success stories, and forums is appropriate and critical, as is understanding their business model and the attendant fees.

You are now aware that new capital is the only rocket fuel that will drive your new venture. Though the road ahead is uncharted, some sign posts are becoming somewhat clearer. However, you must also keep in mind that maximum effort and high measures of good luck and fortune will also be required. National and international events like wars, recessions, and terrorist attacks are now part of the cyclical nature of business affairs. These unforeseen forces can often have the effect of slowing, delaying, or even eradicating the best plans and intentions.

Proper preparation for raising capital is now your number one job.

Once, in Los Alamos, I encountered a team of lab scientists who had most certainly developed God's gift to man in a device called EPPI—a widget they had developed modeled after the ignition box at the head of a nuclear warhead. These folks were bright; they were two couples with huge savings who owned 100% of the common stock, had six PhDs between them, and had been at the Lab since the late 60s. They were committed to making this device, which was the size of a cigar box, available for commercial use. The business plan was in formation, the executive summary done, and the PowerPoint was seductive. However, their marketing strategy was fuzzy, at best.

I accepted their lunch invitation one cold winter day to learn more about EPPI and get to know this new company's four principals. We discussed the venture, how we would raise the $600,000 they needed and how it would be covered. Capital needs can be financed by debt as first option; this is always the least expensive source for the entrepreneur. I suggested that these folks could get mortgages at Los Alamos National Bank on their fully paid homes, since this would be the cheapest capital available.

But they protested, "Mr. Bryant, you do not understand; we do not borrow money and would never consider this option."

So much for that. "Ok," I said, "The other option is equity. You each own 25% and now must share pro-rata for the needed $600,000."

"Mr. Bryant, you are correct; we each own 25% and have no plans to share any ownership percentage with outside investors or your Angels."

Without an offer of debt or equity, their project was dead in the water. Angel investors are not grant providers; they need to get a high return on invested capital for attendant risks. These business owners simply didn't realize that in order to get the capital you need, you have to offer debt in some market rate form to a bank or private lender—or share the equity in your new venture with an Angel Investor.

In later chapters we will discuss capital structures that are most appealing to Angel Investors and the securities documents required to legally accept capital from accredited Angel Investors. New state laws in many states welcome investments of $10,000 or less from unaccredited investors into new ventures. Georgia is in the forefront of this important initiative. Wise legal and accounting advice as you move forward is prudent, intelligent, savvy, and necessary when you are moving past the friends and family stage of corporate financings.

You may worry that debt finance will carry a coupon, interest rate, and that you'll need to make monthly, quarterly, or annual payments on principal. You might assume that equity finance is surely better. This is not the case, however, if your venture is a huge success and the valuation grows. Debt finance carries a fixed or variable coupon but is repaid in an agreed-upon term; after this, the obligation is extinguished and no equity is surrendered. Equity capital for calculation purposes carries an imputed cost of capital of 600 basis points over the T bill rates. Though equity is clearly the more expensive option, it's often the only one open to the entrepreneurial company. Read this paragraph again before you decide how to finance your new venture's capital needs. Rocket fuel in *any* form is expensive.

ACTUAL ANGEL INVESTOR OBSERVATIONS AND COMMENTS

1. If you are looking for a grant, I am not your man.
2. I want and expect a high return on my invested capital. Your offer of 5% is NUTS!
3. Your capital needs are grossly understated; you're going to need two to three times what you're projecting.
4. I need a 40-50% IRR on my risk capital.
5. I am not your parents; I'm an angel Investor looking for a return on my capital in the 40% per year range.
6. I want two to three times on my capital in four to five years.
7. I have the capital you need, but your offering is too complicated. I am just a simple man with two million dollars to invest.
8. Your capital needs are not enough, you will never make it off the runway with $200,000; $500,000 is more realistic.
9. I suggest using a 7A SBA loan for 90% of your capital requirements for your B&B; debt is cheaper than equity.
10. I am good for $100,000 but where is the rest coming from?
11. You have "no skin" in the game to date; why should I take all the upfront risk for 10% of your company?
12. I see that you and your management team have invested

$150,000 and two years of unpaid time in the venture to date. I am impressed. Tell me more...

REFLECTIVE QUESTIONS FOR CHAPTER 4

1. Why is Capital important to your new venture?

   _____

   _____

   _____

2. Where do my future capital requirements come from?

   _____

   _____

   _____

3. Can I delegate the capital raising task to my CFO or others?

   _____

   _____

   _____

4. What are the different forms of Capital?

   _____

   _____

   _____

5. How do I know when I will need more Capital?

   _____

   _____

   _____

5. VALUATION—THE ART OF THE DEAL

NEXT TO THE BUSINESS PLAN, A PROPER AND DEFENSIBLE VALUATION IS one of the most critical elements of the package you'll offer to Angel Investors in your search for seed and early stage capital. *Valuation* tells you, your management team, and any potential investor what your company is worth—not three to five years in the future, but *right now*. It is the seminal event for a young company and is the foundation for how much of the company you will need to sell to get needed capital. It is *not* the "grab the air" event as one Santa Fe entrepreneur demonstrated when I asked him what his company was worth today and how he priced his stock offering: "I have no idea what it is worth; but $1.00 per share seems fair. I have 10 million shares authorized." With no support for his decision or methodology employed to calculate his valuation, he raised over $1 million in capital for his data storage company based on Los Alamos technology.

Valuation done properly—with considerable time and effort—can yield a number that will provide the basis for pricing your common stock or units in your LLC. In the valuation methodology that I use and teach, you'll need 1-3-5 year P&L projections, awareness of industry multiples, and an acceptable discount rate or Internal Rate of Return expected by an Angel Investor. There are many different methodologies in determining valuations; you can use any of them to arrive at a number that is defensible and yet realistically values the young company for pricing this round of capital raising.

Why is valuation important to a young company that may well be pre-revenue? Unlike our Santa Fe Entrepreneur above, most Angel Investors today want to understand the value of the company *today* and then calculate their risk profile before they write a check. Unrealistic projections, inexperienced management teams, and poor business plans all impact the valuation I am asked to perform before one of my young companies presents at my monthly Gathering of Angels.

So with many methodologies for arriving at a proper valuation, how do you select the best one? Some methods are industry specific; my favorite is called Discounted Cash Flow or DCF. When asked to perform a valuation using DCF, I will review the 3-5 year P&L projections for realism and may well discount them at this stage. I then ask for the specific industry Price-Earnings ratio (P/E) and use that number to multiple times the 3rd and 5th year after tax Net Operating Income (NOI). This gives me the future value in year 3 and 5, which I then discount that back to present value with a 40% IRR (discount factor). I then use this number for year 3 and 5 and average the two years. Then I assess the length and strength of the management team assembled by the CEO by analyzing how experienced they are in this space and how many times they have done this before. First time entrepreneurs will get a higher discount and lower valuation. Experienced entrepreneurs deserve a higher valuation and are less likely to make big, and sometimes deadly, mistakes.

It is appropriate and expected for an Angel Investor to ask an Entrepreneur what his company is worth. He'll want to know: what is his valuation? What is his price per share of common stock or units in an LLC? The seasoned Entrepreneur will know the answer and share that with a potential Angel Investor. They'll often negotiate from a fixed number and *not* answer the question by saying, "I don't know." The latter response indicates a lack of sophistication, experiential learning of finance, and will guarantee a valuation done by the Investor at a much lower number than the Entrepreneur would like or deserve. Angel Investors want as much stock as possible for their investment of $50,000 - $100,000 - $200,000; and a higher valuation will suggest fewer shares than a lower valuation. Having a valuation number when dealing with Venture Capitalists (VC) is important as well; however, all VCs will do evaluation calculation, and offer this new—and always lower—number in their issued term sheet. Without a valuation number, you will be required to give away more shares for the same amount of capital that an Angel Investor or VC invests.

Your mission is to quickly raise the amount of seed capital needed for *this round*, trade fewer shares for this capital, and to make sure that you get the fuel needed to get your ship from today till the next round to further expand your business. I advise Entrepreneurs to raise the capital they need *today and for the next six months*; get things done with this capital (this is called hitting milestones) and then come back with another round at a higher valuation. Many companies that are pre-revenue come to the Gathering of Angels and have capital needs of $10M to $15M in the first round after FF&Fs (Friends, Family and Fools). Even with vaulted P&L projections, the young company will need to give away more than 60-75% to raise capital.

I always suggest a series of capital rounds over the first two years of company growth—each round with milestones accomplished and higher corporate valuation and lower cost of capital. Most entrepreneurial CEOs will listen and change their capital requests to a lower number against a lower starting valuation, get the capital needs for six months, and come back later for their next round at a higher valuation.

After the business plan, proper valuation is the heart and soul of providing fuel for your new venture. You need to be prepared to discuss the topic; you cannot just claim to be "a marketing guy," and say that finance is not your long suit. As the CEO of an entrepreneurial company, you must be prepared to both understand valuation and defend the methodology and supporting financial projections you've used.

From your dorm room or the family garage, you have crafted this app or new medical technology and now are ready to offer it to the expectant world and watch the orders flow. You have your Business Plan Executive Summary. You now must price your stock; and valuation is the way you accomplish this. Most Angel Investors will ask for this number to understand what percent of the company they will acquire for their capital invested. As you saw from the comments at the end of the previous chapter, they want their capital returned with a 40-50% IRR for the high risk associated with investing in your venture. (This is called Exit Strategy or a Liquidity Event and will be discussed at length in later chapters of this book.)

Once you calculate your company valuation with assistance and counsel from your advisors and CPA, you then divide the authorized and offered shares by the valuation to arrive at a price per share. If this number is $5 per share and the Angel Investor wants to put in $100,000, you and your corporate Secretary would issue Joe Angel 20,000 shares of stock in your venture. With a supportable and defensible Valuation of $2 Million, Joe Angel would buy .05% of your new company. Even if a local VC has offered $1Million for 75%, you should reject this offer for now. Angel capital is normally less expensive than VC or investment capital.

You'll need this later; it will come as your valuation rises and your cost of capital is reduced.

You should conduct a new Valuation every 90 days—and certainly with every new round of capital. You'll be accomplishing milestones, P&L Projections will change, and management is more seasoned as time and new challenges present themselves. With your board of advisors and board of directors both growing, discounts by investors will be lower as you progress down the capital trail. Once you've raised early capital, you will need to build a strong and industry savvy management team around you. This will influence investment decisions in your favor and get Angel Investors to write you a check—since they tend to put money on the jockey (CEO) more often than the horse (business plan). We'll cover the process of building your management team and advisors with limited resources in detail in later chapters, but for now, understand that it is a critical component in valuation, and is more important than P&L projections.

Valuation is the seminal event in the gestation of the entrepreneurial company. It's the basis of any capital you raise after FF&F or grants you might garner. Do not be caught without a well thought out and reviewed Valuation. Your new venture demands this step if you expect to raise capital from Angel Investors and Venture Capitalists.

REAL LIFE ADVICE AND SUGGESTIONS FROM ANGEL INVESTORS

1. Where is your valuation? (It's basic, but true!).
2. These P&L numbers are from outer space. I will chop them by 50-75%.
3. What methodology did you use to get to this number?
4. I like you, and your company—but this valuation is too high for me.
5. No Pre-revenue company is worth more than $1Million.
6. You need to have a CPA look at your projections.
7. I am afraid of a haircut later on in the next round; can you protect me against dilution?
8. A 7% ROI is not attractive with this high risk venture. Go see your banker at Bank of America, Chase, or Wells Fargo.

9. You need coaching from your CPA or Advisors; these numbers are incredibly unrealistic.
10. I have the money to invest but your valuation is 50% too high. Get your valuation in line and come see me next week.

REFLECTIVE QUESTIONS FOR CHAPTER 5

1. Why is a proper Valuation important to your new venture?

   _____
   _____
   _____

2. This Valuation stuff is complicated! Where can I read more?

   _____
   _____
   _____

3. Why is your Valuation important to Angel Investors and VCs?

   _____
   _____
   _____

4. Is a Valuation done three years ago when you started your venture relevant today?

   _____
   _____
   _____

5. What is the heart and soul of a defensible valuation?

   _____
   _____
   _____

6. PRESENTATION DAY

WITH YOUR NEWLY COMPLETED BUSINESS PLAN, VALUATION CALCULATED, and proper securities documents prepared by a securities lawyer, you are now ready and prepared to present your offering and company to a group of Angel Investors. Your research has indicated that there are five to ten Angel Forums or Clubs across the USA; your job now is to make contact with them and get on the schedule for a future date and venue.

As noted earlier, Angel groups vary in terms of their requirements, entry criteria, and associated fees. Some are more like old investment clubs; these types invest in young companies as a group, employ a high degree of due diligence and conduct member votes on investment decisions. Other groups are like Angel forums: each attendee at Angel meetings will make their own decisions and do their own due diligence before writing a check. Each Angel group has a leader or "Arch Angel" who is responsible for management oversight of the group, setting the venue, arranging the Dance Card of Presenters, and selecting the menu and wine for the evening. Most angel meetings are two to three hours long and held during the week as to not conflict with family obligations on weekends, and are held in private clubs, resorts, or center city hotels.

The Gathering of Angels has held meetings in locales including Santa Fe, Charlotte, Hilton Head, Jacksonville, Tampa, Dallas, Houston, Scottsdale, Carmel, and Orange County. As we recovered from the recession of 2008-2012, Atlanta generated the most Angel checks written to GOA presenting companies—making it my most productive GOA venue.

I've attended over 250 + angel meetings in various cities I watch across the USA as companies seeking capital come to me for funding. If I could understand the concept, business model, could read and understand the business plan, thought the valuation was reasonable, and felt sincerely that my assembled group of Angel Investors would enjoy hearing from a particular company, I invite them to present at my next GOA meeting. Normally, the leader of an Angel group starts the vetting process for presenters and other members with industry expertise will assist and give guidance and sage advice. This process normally takes one to five days. If approved for presentation, the company is offered a presenter slot at a future meeting.

Most people find me by making initial contact via our GOA website; sometimes they call or email. Most will say they are looking for seed capital and have exhausted their savings, their family and friends have stopped returning their calls, and now they need to meet some Angel Investors. When they ask whether I can help them, my first response is "maybe." I require them to send their business plan, executive summary, and a PowerPoint if they have one. I will review these items and evaluate whether they'd be successful with my Angel Forum. Typically, 40-50% of the submissions are incomplete and more work is needed before an invitation is extended to present at a future GOA meeting.

Preparation is high priority; it's absolutely mandatory to have all needed items with you when you present. I suggest that all presenters come armed for battle and dressed for success. Showing up in blue jeans, sweater and flip flops is not acceptable; a suit or sport coat, slacks and tie or pant suit or dress for the ladies are required. I tell each GOA presenter to arrive at 2PM for three hours of intensive training and practice before they present that evening from 5-8pm. This practice session is mandatory, even though they have been vetted by me and have paid their GOA presentation fee. Without it, they do not present that evening. Even the most assured and seasoned presenters must undergo this step; it's a vital one for our process.

So let's say you have received an invitation to come to Atlanta Gathering of Angels to present your technology company with a novel solution for electronic medical records storage and recovery. You are located in Dallas but most of the Texas Angels and VCs seem to be more interested in medical devices and software. Atlanta is a short 1.5 hour flight and you plan to arrive by noon on the night of the GOA event. You have prepared a twenty slide PowerPoint presentation that hits all the hot buttons most Angel Investors will be wondering about. I have reviewed your deck of slides and made four suggestions that you have incorporated and revised. You have prepared and dropped your five-page executive summary into the suggested one-page Executive summary model provided. You plan to use the back for photos of your novel process and four shots of your exceptional management team. At GOA, we provide a template called the Diamics model for a very tight executive summary—something you found most helpful and instructive.

You have been asked to bring forty copies of the new summary on hard stock paper with light lamination (since Angels often spill red wine on the GOA event tables and lamination saves your material). You also come to GOA with ten to twelve full business plans for most interested Angel Investors to accelerate the due diligence process and shorten the time from your GOA presentation to check writing by your new Angel Investor. The normal period of due diligence by an Angel Investor is one to fifteen; however, it can be longer if you need to provide later material or if you show up unprepared to the GOA meeting. Business cards are also suggested.

A very tight one page front and back Executive Summary is critical to your ability to raise capital from Angel Investors. Normally, this should be the first part of your business plan. However, I've reviewed some business plans that have this as a five to ten page synopsis of all that is covered. If the summary is presented in this way, the Angel Investor will read only those five pages—not the full business plan. Before presentation at a monthly meeting of the Gathering of Angels, I email all presenters a very tight one pager that I suggest they employ. It is a model I adapted from one of my early GOA presenters, and it tells everything necessary—about the company, the opportunity, solution, products, target market, market size, projected financials in snapshot format, key management, full contact info, funds sought, CAP structure, and company website. I tell anyone who has five pages to compress it into one page with photos of the management team, a one line brief, and then photos of their product or service.

Angel Investors are busy people with fairly short attention spans who are sometimes sitting through one presentation after another. This new venture must be compelling and complete and catch their interest within a few minutes—if not seconds—of reading. The shorter, the better; the more concisely you can get your point across, they more likely you are to get noticed.

Preparing to present to Gathering of Angels is hard work, and the Executive Summaries are an essential component. These are provided under the presenter GOA Dance Card to each attendee at the Gathering of Angels; they are in front of the Angel Investors as they sit and listen to each of the presenters. Angel Investors will rarely take the time to read the entire document; instead, they'll peruse succinct one pagers and use these as the basis for questions and to get better understanding. Arriving at the GOA meeting without a one-page summary will most assuredly reduce a presenter's chances of raising the needed capital that evening.

Not only is a Gathering of Angels meeting a unique opportunity to raise capital; it's also a teaching process. It provides information on the discipline Entrepreneurs need to have to raise capital, not only from GOA Angel Investors but all those you meet going forward. After years of preparing and attending such meetings, I can usually predict who is ready. Most often, those are the ventures that get funded and join my growing list of GOA success stories.

Though the Executive summary is required for GOA meetings, it continues to have value after this event. It is good business to have 100-150 of these printed and with you at any time; then, you're always ready to share them with potential Angel Investors. One presenter from Greenville didn't have any takers after an Atlanta Gathering of Angels. But she had prepared her tight Diamics model Executive Summary and compelling twenty slide PowerPoint, and had her security documents in place. So three weeks later, when she met her Angel Investor over coffee in her hometown, her prior GOA preparation led to a $250,000 check. She then thanked me for the preparation, coaching, and guidance.

You will have practiced your twenty minute presentation ten or more times before the GOA practice session—certainly before the actual GOA event. It's always a good plan to time yourself to insure you stay inside the guidelines of twenty minutes. Going over often will cut into your time for follow-up questions. Most Angel groups like the Gathering of Angels encourage a thirty minute social time before the session formally begins to allow Angel Investors to meet and greet the presenters before hearing them present. Most often, the Angel Investors enjoy a light supper and have a glass of wine or two. A charity auction or fund raiser has never been successful without a large budget for red and white wines optional. And we make sure that soft drinks are always available for non-drinkers' enjoyment.

The twenty slide PowerPoint needs to be done professionally and show that you've put considerable time and concentrated effort into it. Creations that have obviously been thrown together at the last minute show poorly and attract little investment interest. It is fine to embed videos in the presentation, but bear in mind that switching presentation packages causes delays, and as Bill Gates can certainly attest, your intended audience is lost and often rejects your important message.

You should plan on a seamless twenty minute presentation that is well practiced and rehearsed, with information in large font, photos on each page, free of long wordy paragraphs.

PowerPoint can be a tricky tool; bullet points and lengthy paragraphs with six-point fonts are not recommended. The best approach is to include one to three slides at the front to describe the product or service and immediately catch the interest and attention of the Angel Investors in the room. Follow that up with one to two slides on the current management team, with future slots to be filled in once you receive funding. One slide might display pictures of the current board of advisors and board of directors.

These slides are critical early in your presentation; they give the eagerly listening Angel Investors confidence that you have assembled an impressive team around you as CEO and will pull this deal off regardless of the challenges you face. Remember the horse/jockey rule we introduced earlier: people bet on the Jockey 75% of the time, not what horse he/she is riding that day. The same holds true for young Entrepreneurial companies. A seasoned battle scarred CEO who has made many mistakes, learned from these errors and missteps, and survived to fight another day is 50% more likely to get Angel Investor money than a first time entrepreneur.

Your Presentation should also include one to two slides on the financials with snapshot *summaries only*; there's no need to include a full and detailed chart of accounts down to the penny. A well done snapshot will include revenues, costs and net profit for 1-3-5 years, and margins. Then you'll want to show one or two slides on the offering specifics, capital sought in this round of finance, use of funds, and minimum investment. The exit strategy or liquidity event planned for early investors is of paramount interest and deserves a full slide. Even though you may be looking for $600,000 to $700,000 in capital, I suggest a minimum investment in the $25,000 to $50,000 range to attract the smaller Angel Investor. Those with deeper pockets and larger appetites will suggest larger amounts of investment interest.

Every presentation needs a closing summary slide with five to six points that summarize the entire presentation. After presenting this last slide of the evening, do not close with, "Are there any questions?" A good salesman should *never* close with this line! You are asking for money; your goal is to secure another meeting with an interested Angel Investor who can write a check to help you sustain or launch your new venture. I recommended that you end by walking away from the podium, looking the audience in the eyes, and saying something like, "Thank you for your genuine interest and high attention tonight. I need your help to make my dream a reality. If you would like to know more about XYZ Company and meet with me privately, I am available tonight after this meeting or all day tomorrow. Fill in the GOA Evaluation Forms for timely follow up. Thank you."

Your chance at the brass ring is limited to a precious time period; proper preparation and practice is mandatory. Only you and the Angel group leader will know if you have truly done everything necessary. You will be able to gauge the audience's reaction via the Evaluation Sheets that each Angel Investor receives and fills out, normally within two to three minutes after the presentation. Angels are required to fill out these forms, which are then given to the presenting GOA Entrepreneur. He/she also receives end copies of the RSVP List, Registration List, and copies of all attendee business cards. Business cards are solicited at the GOA registration desk. This allows all the Angels in attendance to have access to clear and printed contact information for each presenter. Immediate follow up, contact, conference calls, and meetings are mandatory for capital funding. Delayed response and following up two to three weeks later after GOA event is unacceptable—and rarely productive.

REAL LIFE OBSERVATIONS AND COMMENTS FROM ANGEL INVESTORS

1. Your presentation was excellent but I never heard from you for three weeks. Your lack of follow-up caused me to lose interest on your venture.
2. You left out any mention of the management team. I invest in the Jockey, not the horse! I need more information on the people on your team.
3. You read every line in the presentation; it put me to sleep.
4. Your financial slides were too detailed and fonts were too tiny. I could barely make out any information.
5. You failed to get my high interest and attention in the first sixty seconds.
6. Your faded logo tee shirt was cute but out of place for this Angel event. Do you own a sport coat or suit?

7. Your white shoes are nice; but this is not a 60's night club.

8. Your presentation was not clear, which shows that you did not practice enough!

9. Having your team in the room was supportive, but you need to use them during the presentation.

10. You have had too much to drink and embarrassed us all.

11. If you have all the money you claim to have, why are you here presenting tonight, asking us for ours?

12. Your financial projections are completely off.

13. Without a tight Executive Summary, I am not interested.

14. This summary is ten pages long; I don't have the time or attention span to read it.

15. Nice Summary—but you left out your management team and capital sought.

16. I have money to invest and this summary is tight and professionally prepared; I am in!

17. You followed the GOA Model and this looks good. I am interested; show me more.

18. Show me everything quickly; if I want more, I will ask.

19. This Summary is intriguing; send me your full Business Plan for my review.

20. Bravo! I am intrigued & interested. Let's meet tonight!

REFLECTIVE QUESTIONS FOR CHAPTER 6

1. Is lots of prior practice important to my success on Presentation Day? How and when will I practice?

   _____
   _____
   _____

2. Can you just wing it on Presentation Day and talk from the heart?

   _____
   _____
   _____

3. What documents do I need on Presentation Day?

_____

_____

_____

4. My PowerPoint is fifty slides of marketing information. Does that sound okay?

    _____

    _____

    _____

5. My Executive Summary is twelve pages long—is that okay?

    _____

    _____

    _____

6. What are the seven essential elements of a well-crafted Executive Summary?

    _____

    _____

    _____

7. Is it okay if I skip the Practice sessions? I do this all the time.

    _____

    _____

    _____

8. Will you ever revise the Executive Summary?

    _____

    _____

    _____

7. THE CAPITAL PLAN

NOW THAT YOU HAVE PRESENTED AT THE RECENT GATHERING OF ANGELS event, it is time to set up your Capital Plan for the next three years. *But, you might wonder, how can I plan that far in advance when I only started my venture six months ago?* It's a daunting thought, for sure, but capital is the force that keeps you going. As you grow, add staff and management team members, open new locations and expand your foot print, you will need more capital. Raising the seed round of 300-500K after the friends and family round is underway and this infusion of capital will get you 6-9 months into your business plan. While your valuation might be low today, this will change once you raise the capital and hit your milestones.

With good forward momentum and a growing management team that's focused and 100% committed to growing the venture, you should begin planning and laying out your Capital Plan. This will project your capital needs for the next three years. Each time you raise more capital, your future becomes a bit clearer—sometimes allowing you to avert cash crunches. With these infusions of rocket fuel and the accomplishment of milestones, increased sales, new customers, new product offerings, enlargement of your Board of Advisors and Board of Directors, new discussions ongoing with Venture Capitalists and Investment Bankers, your world has become more exciting and always unpredictable.

You are beginning to realize that raising capital is a full time job that you now have in addition to running the venture that you founded. You get more done with each passing day and each round of finance, and the business plan of 6-8 months ago is constantly changing. You're thankful you didn't have your business plan bound. Putting it into a three-ringed binder was the best approach, since you've as altered it no less than ten times and are anticipating even more changes coming next week.

As time progresses and you begin to think about your next round of finance, you and your newly hired CFO (chief financial officer) should consider all sources of capital and seek the lowest cost selection—or what I call the Optimum Capital Structure. You began with some capital from your own bank account, and with some loans from family members—and then an Angel seed round of 200K from the Gathering of Angels. It might be time to look again at debt capital from a local bank as this is unquestionably the cheapest sources of capital for a young company. A bank loan at prime + 3% is considerably less expensive than equity capital that I calculate at current T-Bills + 600 basis points. True cost of capital is revealing and should be considered and discussed with each round of capital raising.

Each round from your interactions with Angel—often called the Seed and Early stage rounds—will require proper Securities documents. This might include a Subscription Agreement, a Private Placement Memorandum (PPM), a Term Sheet, and often registration with state and even the Federal SEC. Audited financials may be required at later rounds so it is important to keep financials current with Quick Books or Quicken (not just in a shoe box.) I have seen offers of equity finance fall apart because the entrepreneurial venture was not keeping adequate books and records. On day one, you should buy a software package, do the posting to your chart of accounts and produce monthly P&L and balance sheet statements. If accounting is not your longest suit, find support or take a class and learn Quick Books. Good securities and accounting advice early and often can assure that your progress remains within state and federal guidelines and statutes as you move through your capital plan.

You also want to carefully select a qualified attorney and accountant to do your Subscription Agreement and PPM. While these can be costly hires, you will be able to pay this talent back in stock, trade out, or out of capital raised in the next round on occasion. Creative finance is a critical aspect of dealing with the talented professionals you need to grow your business. Your focus should be on finding an individual or firm that specializes in young entrepreneurial ventures—not Fortune 500 companies. You may be there later on but now you just need talent and expertise—fast, reliable, and on the cheap.

Capital Plans like Business Plans are forever a moving target and subject to weekly, even daily review and modifications. The new marketing budget is more costly than earlier projected; you underestimated the legal costs of entering China; your new CEO demands a signing bonus and will come on board *if* you pay for his relocation expenses; the list goes on. You can never plan for surprises like these, but they do occur—and will change any business and/or capital plan. Contingencies in most budgets can cover some of these unexpected events—but never all.

Implementation of Plan B and Plan C are assured as you move down the business trail to growing your venture. Plans are just plans; they'll always be subject to revisions and modifications. Much as we like to believe they can, budgets and projections cannot predict the future. Only as time passes and reality sets in, challenges are met and overcome, the smoke clears—and the final results revealed.

Like your Business Plan, you should keep your Capital Plan stored in both a binder and on your hard drive—places that keep it accessible to change and recurring modification. You'll be conducting an ongoing search for the lowest cost of capital from various sources—and market forces and FED actions will keep this search challenging. What worked last year is rarely the best option for the next round of finance. Your well educated, seasoned and experienced CFO will guide you through this process of raising capital. He or she is someone you can consider not just your green-eyed, bean counting back office person—but your full partner in the ongoing capital raising process.

Remember that you need to redo your valuation with each successive round of finance and milestone accomplishments. You'll doubtlessly be able to increase and adjust upwards, thus lowering your overall cost of capital. As time consuming as this process is, creating and following your Capital Plan is smart business—and guarantees constant modifications. A well thought out plan will be reviewed by most sources of finance in each successive round.

ACTUAL ANGEL INVESTOR ADVICE AND COMMENTS

1. Show me your Capital Plan and sources of capital since inception.
2. What is your cost of capital?
3. What is your valuation today vs. last year?
4. Count on me in the next round, but not this one. I want to see more forward progress and milestones achieved.
5. I was in your last round, but I am tapped out now.
6. Did you look at a 7A SBA Loan instead of giving up all this precious equity?
7. Why not use debt finance for that building or lease space and not tie up precious capital?
8. I like your new CFO; he understands finance and

accounting and has prepared this well. I am in this round for $1Million

9. As a VC, I need to review your Capital Plan, Valuation, and full Business Plan. Without access to all three, I am not interested.

10. The fact that you've done your Securities Docs in proper order for this current round is very important to me. Count me in for $500K. Using expensive equity capital to pay off cheap long term debt is not good business sense.

11. What is your Optimum Capital Structure today?

REFLECTIVE QUESTIONS FOR CHAPTER 7

1. Why is a capital plan important and relevant?

2. I need 10M now to get my venture launched. Is this what I should ask for now and in my first round of finance?

3. What is my lowest cost of capital?

4. Who can assist me in the creation of my capital plan?

5. Are 1-3-5 year P&L projections important in the creation of a realistic capital plan?

8. EXIT STRATEGY FOR EARLY INVESTORS

YOU'VE NOW HAD SUCCESS AT THE GATHERING OF ANGELS AND HAVE FIVE Angel investors who want to be involved in your new company. Three have invested 50K each, one for $100,000, and another for $250,000. You are certainly a GOA Success Story, and have truly made some strides since that original $100,000 your parents loaned. Now you have to begin planning for an exit strategy or a liquidity event for those that join you as Angel investors from the GOA meeting.

You're probably curious about why you have to plan for an exit for them so soon. While the people who lent you money during the first round of raising capital are more patient and will support you without some hope and prayer for liquidity, most Angel Investors—and all VCs and Investment Bankers—are a different breed. They're excited to invest in the next Microsoft or Apple, but want in 2-4 years an exit from your rocket ship at a substantial IRR on invested capital. Investors beyond that initial round are *investors*—not relatives. And they need to know your exit plan.

Angel Investors will hear your PPT presentation, read your executive summary and then your business plan, meet with you and your management team several times, check your references, and confirm paying customers and new channels of distribution. Then, they will pass 90% of the time or pull the trigger and write a check. Once they join the ranks of investors in your company, your job as CEO and entrepreneur is to consider them as part of your extended family. You must keep them posted on your progress monthly or quarterly, review your monthly financials, and call on them for advice as needed. You must remain assertive and keep their excitement alive. Your role is to ensure they're always informed about your company and its forward progress.

What does an Exit Strategy look like? Acceptable exits might include a buy back by Management with a defined ROI. This is easy and will bring smiles to your Angel Investors pocket books. How long should you wait for liquidity? If you offer 7-10 years to Angel Investors that they will be repaid, your investment will not attract capital. But 2-5 years is in range and a 30-50% IRR is in the market range for seed and early stage investments. Most Angel Investors know that every investment will not produce this; their experience tells them that many will not make it and such a high return reflects higher-risk investments. With your capital secured and in the bank, your job is to get paying customers, build your management team and check off some milestones. You are now planning for the next round of capital and—as you remember from Chapter 5— now is the time to consider a new valuation. Your good progress should raise this number and reduce your cost of capital. Some of your investors are good for some period; some may want out in your next round, if someone acquires you, or if you take the company public. Every investor is different, and each one needs your individual attention and nurturing. Monthly, or at minimum quarterly, calls or emails to your entire investor pool will keep you abreast of their exit interests, motivations, and support.

Most Angel Investors will hang in with you for two to four years. But with each passing quarter and forward progress, they will begin to ask when you will liquidate their precious investment. Many young companies are acquired at high multiples; acquisition is the most likely exit for most investors and as far as most Angels are concerned, it cannot come soon enough. If you have raised your company profile and gotten more new paying customers each month, you will appear on the radar screen for the big fish in your pond. Many will be public companies who need to acquire to grow—and you might become a target. Perhaps you have a situation where your technology is unique, management team is exceptional, paying customers love the offering, and breakeven is three quarters away. You are beginning to realize that you are a code writer and start-up genius at heart—not a big corporate VP for Google or IMB. An early exit does not sound too bad; the capital on an acquisition would have appeal to all your investors and would seed your next new venture. You might even dream at night of the serenity of a yacht sailing in the Bahamas that has your name on the stern plate.

Depending on the economic cycle, the Initial Public Offering (IPO) is either a bonanza or heartbreak. It will likely be very costly and time-consuming; Investment Bankers will work their magic, get your stock placed and collect reasonable fees for their efforts. Compliance issues and regulatory filings are huge; life as a public company is only for the strong and seasoned veterans of earlier battles. Reverse mergers into public shells are another method for getting your company to the public market; however, they rarely offer investment banker support and requisite capital needed. Most of my GOA presenting companies that have used this method to become a public traded company now regret the move; they bemoan the compliance and regulator costs, and have little to show for this most seductive public-traded adventure. Their advice to a new CEO would be to stay clear of reverse mergers into clean public shells, as this exit strategy tends to guarantee many grey—and even white—hairs.

You cannot plan your Exit Strategy alone; it demands many hours of discussion and debate with your CFO, Management team, Board of Advisors, and your Board of Directors. All of these individuals will vote on your final decision. This will be a long and difficult journey if you are hard headed, obdurate, obstinate, and un-coachable. You absolutely must involve and allow advice from your CPA and outside legal team; these are the experts in this space whose experience your must consider and respect. Without them, you cannot advance. They have traveled this road before; you have not. You must put your intellect and oversized ego in check, listen closely to advice and wise counsel offered—and let your Board of Directors guide you toward the right and final decision. Miss-steps at this stage in the game can be dangerous—even fatal.

If you do it right by rewarding your early Angel Investors with a reasonable exit strategy and liquidation event, they most certainly will be happy and satisfied that they made the right decision at that Gathering of Angels meeting two years ago. They'll look back and realize that choosing to invest 100K in your company was the right thing to do. Now after two years, they'll enjoy an Exit, as you are considering a serious offer to buy your company at a valuation that is two times your current numbers. Your Board is engaged and you are stoked. This is a big payday for you, your parents, and your early Angel Investors. You doze off and prepare for the battles that await in the morning when you meet with your SEC-trained lawyers, CPA, and Investment Bankers.

ACTUAL ANGEL INVESTOR ADVICE AND COMMENTS

1. What is your exit strategy for my investment?
2. I am not part of your extended family; I need to get 40-50% IRR on invested capital…give me specifics on how this is going to happen.

3. I like your plan, but an IPO is a pipe dream for a company of your size.
4. Without customers, you have no hope for an exit for me.
5. I like your plan and management team; tell me your Exit Strategy.
6. An exit strategy in 7-10 years is not appealing to me; I might be dead by then!

REFLECTIVE QUESTIONS FOR CHAPTER 8

1. My family and friends do not care if I repay their investment; why would an Angel Investor?

    _____
    _____
    _____

2. What are three to four common Exit Strategies for an Angel Investor?

    _____
    _____
    _____

3. What is the ROI expected by an Angel Investor?

    _____
    _____
    _____

4. I will pay Prime + 3% at my local bank for debt capital. Is this an acceptable ROI for an Angel Investor?

    _____
    _____
    _____

5. Who can help me craft an attractive Exit Strategy for an Angel Investor?

    _____
    _____
    _____

9. NETWORKING 101 AND CIVIC RENT

YOU HAVE JOINED THE RANKS OF THE ENTREPRENEURS, AND NOW YOUR days are full with planning and preparation for your new exciting venture. Your family still needs your attention, of course; but since you're still working out of your home, you see them often. You might explore the local small business incubator and that new fancy accelerator that just opened five miles away sometime in the future (we'll discuss both of these in detail in Chapter 13). For now, you have decided that the best option is to work somewhere that does not have a rent component (besides your normal mortgage payment.)

However, you will realize after a few months operating out of your basement that it does get lonely—and you'll miss the camaraderie and fellowship of co-workers. Your dog, Maggie, sleeps at your feet and Felix, the cat, comes to visit and see what is going on, but it's not the same. Additionally, the fact that you're at home makes you more accessible for pressing family responsibilities. It will eventually become clear that you need to be out and about, telling the story of your new company to potential customers, investors, and service providers that can help you become the success your deserve.

Fortunately for you, every city of substantial size has 5-15 business and networking meetings per day—opportunities for you to meet and greet people who can be helpful to you and your new venture. It won't be long before you come to see networking as one of those *survival skills* that you need to put major effort behind—something that will pay large dividends to you and your venture. I call this chapter **Networking 101 and Civic Rent** because the basics of getting out and meeting people who can help your survive and prosper is not just important; it's absolutely *critical* if you plan to make it in the rough, uncharted seas of entrepreneurial life.

Most large cities have chapters of the Jaycees or Junior Chamber of Commerce. The Atlanta Jaycees was the first organization I joined when

I first returned to Atlanta after my Vietnam service—and after five years as a member, I became president and was running the weekly meetings. At that time, we had 300 young men from small, medium, and large companies who were on the move upward and who all wanted to meet, greet, and help each other succeed in the business world. As president, this also gave me a seat on the Board of Directors of the Atlanta Chamber of Commerce. This latter group truly was all the movers and shakers in the Atlanta community and the most wonderful networking opportunity a young man of 27 years old could imagine. This position gave me an office in downtown Atlanta on Marietta Street, a Jaycee secretary, and use of a complimentary new Pontiac car for my Jaycee year. Though it also came with its share of meetings and obligations, the time expended was more than worth it. My confidence level grew, and my contacts were broad and deep.

Networking can lead to many exciting opportunities and open doors you might have never imagined. One good thing led to another, which led to another. If you can find an area of interest and give your time and talents to that organization or charity, you will meet folks along the way that can help you grow as a person—and help your business prosper.

Everywhere I volunteered and attended meetings, I made new friends from whom I learned many life lessons. After some time, I had built a friendship web of contacts that has lasted a lifetime—something that never would have been possible if I had stayed in my office on the Northeast Expressway. Though it might seem as though the best thing for your businesses is to stay "hunkered down" and focused, you have to get out there and *make connections.*

When I first returned from Vietnam, I also began a search for mentors. I found the then Chairman and CEO of Citizens and Southern National Bank, Mills B Lane, through the Atlanta Jaycees. Mr. Lane had grown up in the banking business his father started in Savannah. As busy as Mr. Lane was, he always had time for ambitious young men and women who sought his wise advice and counsel. He always welcomed my calls and gave me sage guidance whenever I would come by for a visit.

Mr. Lane also taught me the value of paying your "Civic Rent" in the community where you live. That means giving not only of your money to various organizations in need, but giving your time and talents as well. He told me, "If you aspire to sit at the table of leadership and make a real difference in your community, you must pay your Civic Rent." I took Mr. Lane's wise words to heart. It would benefit you to do the same.

If you are a member of a local religious community, you'll find opportunities to contribute and make connection there, as well. Such institutions function normally with small underpaid but talented staffs, along with countless legions of volunteers who give of their time and talents. As you join these ranks of the volunteers, you will meet folks who are supporting a collective mission and make long-lasting friendships. You'll spend a lot of time enjoying those "good feelings" that come when you devote time and talents to a worthwhile cause or matter that's close to your heart.

Networking can also extend to your local educational institutions or your alma mater. Most colleges and universities, and even some high schools, have extensive alumni networks of which you can become a part at any point in life. If you're currently working on an undergraduate degree or MBA, classmates might be the key to crucial business contacts. We all have different skill sets, interests, and experiences; a classmate in your finance class who works for a local bank might be able to provide that key introduction when your new venture needs a bank loan. Folks that you meet in class or over late dinner can become part of your network and may help you in the future, if not right away. A good data base system like Outlook or software program like ACT will insure that you can recall them when the need arises.

REAL LIFE ANGEL INVESTOR SUGGESTIONS AND ADVICE

1. Get out of the garage, Sam, and into the mainstream of business in your city.
2. I see you everywhere, George; you're really making a difference in our community.
3. You did well with the last fundraiser; would you consider becoming a club officer?
4. I like your style and confidence, tell me more about your new venture.
5. You were impressive as an officer. I need a VP of Sales; are you interested?
6. My daughter is coming out of college and maybe she could be an intern in your new business.
7. Your new venture might be a fit for my public traded company. Can we talk merger in the New Year?

8. I like your positive attitude and you get things done, I want to invest in your company now!

REFLECTIVE QUESTIONS FOR CHAPTER 9

1. Why should I leave my garage or basement office? It seems like I'm getting a lot done there.

    _____
    _____
    _____

2. Where can I meet other like-minded entrepreneurs?

    _____
    _____
    _____

3. I need capital for growing my business. Will Angel Investors find me and come to my garage office?

    _____
    _____
    _____

4. I will give back to my community and my church when I have more time and money. Is that enough?

    _____
    _____
    _____

5. My family and close friends are tapped out. Where do I find Angel Investors?

    _____
    _____
    _____

10. MANAGEMENT TEAM

IN ADDITION TO A STRONG AND TENACIOUS CEO, THE MANAGEMENT TEAM in an entrepreneurial company is a key element to the venture's ultimate success or failure in every industry or market space. Without a supportive team surrounding him or her, few solo CEOs will stand the test when the winds of change and turbulence blow. A strong, supportive management team that a CEO and his Board carefully select can often restructure and modify a weak venture, allowing it to live to fight another day.

When I vet companies to present at the Gathering of Angels, I look primarily at the CEO and his/her management team—*then* the concept, product or service. I weight the management team at 40% weighted when I do my early review. I like to get to know the CEO or Chairman or both, but also meet as many members of the management team as possible to build my confidence that the venture will be both well received by my angel investors and have a reasonable chance of survival. I get proposals every week from solo CEOs with a great idea, an invention and maybe even a patent on some earth shattering widget—but without any sort of a team to support them. I suggest that these CEOs return in several months after assembling and working together with a team that's achieving milestones and acquiring paying customers.

Business plans and PowerPoints will change, so every entrepreneur needs support from a flexible, adaptable, and adroit management team that will aid them in making these changes. Seed and early stage business ventures are high risk and deserve a high rate of return for early investors. Angels and VCs alike should always look first at the CEO and then the management team assembled to execute the plan. Venture Capitalists do spend considerable time interviewing and reference checking the management team assembled by the CEO. Though it's tempting, convenient, and most assuredly cost effective, having family members as part of your team isn't always the proper approach—or one that inspires confidence from potential investors in your venture. It's often the case that your parents put up the early money, but unless they bring talent and skills to the table, they should remain in your investor files and not on the management team. Husband and wife teams are OK, but certainly not as professional as a strong management team that's you've pulled together based on skills and experience.

The CEO must convene the management team; this isn't something that HR can do, as is often the case in bigger organizations. The entrepreneurial company rarely has an HR department anyway; this is just another task the CEO must handle, along with many others. A seasoned entrepreneur will know and recognize his/her skills, be able to tell what's lacking, and use that information to decide what other management team members to bring on board. Finance, marketing, sales, business development, product/service development are all areas of specialty and slots on the team you must fill as the venture grows and expands.

You might be wondering how one might pay for this talent and retain them once hired. Cash in the seed and early stage ventures is always tight; unless you're able to raise sufficient capital early, some of the team will need to wait for proper funding to join your management team. Some older, seasoned folks might agree to join and wait to receive payment until you're able to raise the necessary capital. Others might work for stock and join for the excitement and the thrill of the chase. Options and warrants are also methods of compensations when cash is precious—or non-existent. Even here, my earlier comments about family members holds true; you can fill interim positions with senior family members who do, in fact, have the needed skills until you have the funds to allow full time hires.

When selecting members of your management team, it's of course the best option to pick those that have skills that you do not possess and that compliment your talents and areas of strength. You have a large and complex job to do as the CEO; oversight and leadership of the management team is paramount. You *set the tone* for the entrepreneurial corporation; but your team must *execute your vision* and perform assigned tasks. If they don't, you must replace them. Management teams are fluid and flexible by design. They often expand or contract based on available capital and current business conditions. There have been many instances where I previewed a management team and then saw new players in various slots one to two years later. Seasoned CEOs will often bring trusted lieutenants from one venture on to the next opportunity, since some perform well in various kinds of environments. Not all endeavors will be Facebook success stories; but strong management teams increase the company's chance at entering new markets, acquiring new customers, and surviving and enduring the first five years of entrepreneurial life.

When preparing my presenters at the monthly Gathering of Angels meetings, I often talk about how important the CEO or Jockey is. Certainly a solid horse, good trainer, and no injuries contribute to the potential victory.. Build your management team with thought and creative finance and prepare for battle with talented folks at your side who are fully committed to accomplishing your vision.

ANGEL INVESTOR COMMENTS AND OBSERVATIONS

1. What happens if you get hit by a train? Show me your Management Team.
2. I know you have exhausted your personal savings but you need to surround yourself with a talented team, and I don't see it.
3. Your mother loves you and always will—but she should not be your COO.
4. I have money to invest and like you—but I don't like your management team. I will pass.
5. Why not use stock or options to attract a longer management team; I did when I started my 3rd venture.
6. I will invest 400K in your venture but you need a COO. I will step in for 12 months and help you run this company. Deal?
7. Add three more folks to your management team and I will invest 200K.

REFLECTIVE QUESTIONS FOR CHAPTER 10

1. Why should I have a management team around me as CEO?

    _____

    _____

    _____

2. Who should I have as members of my management team? What areas of expertise do I need?

_____

_____

_____

3. Is being the Lone Ranger a good practice for entrepreneurial companies?

_____

_____

_____

4. Where can I find the talent needed for my management here in this small town?

_____

_____

_____

5. Who should I NOT have as members of my management team?

_____

_____

_____

11. BOARDS AND ADVISORS

AS DISCUSSED IN THE PRIOR CHAPTER, AN EXPERIENCED ENTREPRENEUR-
ial CEO will assemble his/her management team with high purpose,
and will give considerable thought assigning tasks for accomplishing the
company's mission. Equally important to the team is the quality and
quantity of members of the company Board of Directors and Board of
Advisors, along with talented and committed legal and accounting assistance. Without the proper oversight and guidance, a management team
can drift and lose their way. The true purpose of these boards and advisors is to keep the people at the helm of these young companies on
track. Corporate structure requires that the CEO report to the Board of
Directors—something that's most crucial from early days as the company grows, and even more so as it matures. The larger the young company
gets, the more critical oversight and seasoned and trusted advice can be.

The Board of Directors is the governing body; its members can hire and
fire management and offer direction and focus to the team that you have
assembled. Your job as CEO is to execute the plans that your board has
agreed upon and approved and keep them informed on major issues, capital
needs, and challenges. The role of the Board is not to *run* the venture's daily
activities, but to offer wise and relevant advice and counsel and approve
major capital projects the management team has recommended.

Choosing your Board is like selecting your management team, in
that it is a critical step for your success as a new venture. In corporate
America, the Board of Directors is the authoritative element in the overall
governance of the young company. It is responsible for policy, direction,
and oversight. The Chair of the Board of Directors is selected by vote
of the Board. He or she runs the meetings and is your coach while in
the chair. Five to seven smart and committed folks need to serve as your
initial Board. As CEO, you should be one of them.

Major shareholders and large investors will and should demand a seat here; but a diversified board will make for better decision making. Clones of you and your style are not suggested for inclusion, and you should opt for family members with great caution. I like to see a senior executive with lots of knowledge and expertise in the company's industry fill the position of Chair. Other board members will have their areas of high expertise and need to be contributors of time and resources; otherwise, you have no choice but to ask them to step down.

It can be difficult to determine how you compensate this board when cash is tight and every dollar counts. Cash flow is always at a premium for the young company and director's fees of 50-100K are a pipe dream until you reach a later and healthier stage in your growth. As with your management team, company stock and/or stock options and warrants are responsible methods of payment, and deferred compensation until cash flow warrants is also acceptable. You expect their time, intellect, and full commitment to your venture from your Board of Directors; up front agreement is required. They must buy into your vision and feel that they can contribute to your success.

It's advisable to hold monthly board meetings during early days, as things often happen so quickly that quarterly or annual meetings are not sufficient to provide proper oversight and guidance. Often a Board of Directors is charged with removal of the CEO, something that should not come as a shock to you. They are there to guide and assist you; however, they are ultimately responsible to the shareholders and by law must re-elect them on an annual basis at shareholder meetings. Limiting terms of service to three years is constructive and provides new ideas and perspective to healthy board decision making.

Your new Board of Advisors is also important as you grow your entrepreneurial business. These folks should always have a great deal of experience and serve as a sounding board for ideas and provide advice on entering new markets and undertaking new initiatives. They may later join your Board of Directors. Like your Board of Directors, folks need to be of high intellect, impeccable integrity, and have deep industry knowledge and contacts. I suggest that this group consist of five to fifteen folks who, like your main board, you can pay in stock or options. Only when one is needed for a specific involved project or initiative, would you need to compensate in precious cash.

The selection process is thorough and requires your time and diligence. You'll want to conduct background checks since investors—and the business world at large—will judge you by the people with which you surround yourself. The longer and stronger both of these boards become, the easier it will be for you to attract capital. Other Board members, and your management team, can help you in this search for talent.

Selecting your law firm and specific attorney is another crucial decision in your entrepreneurial journey. You need someone who can draw corporate documents, file patents, offer corporate tax advice and—if need be—defend you in court. Lawyers today all have his/her specialties, which can make it both easy and challenging to find the best to suit your needs. Many firms today are willing to work with entrepreneurs whom they know cannot pay the normal hourly or retainers that bigger firms can afford. I have found over time that often the biggest firms will have rates and payment plans for their entrepreneurial clients. They remember how Bill Gates offered an Albuquerque law firm stock for pennies a share—but they said no and demanded payment in cash. We all know how that story turned out! Pick the best lawyer for your industry and be creative with his/her compensation. They are a valuable part of your management team.

Finding the right and most helpful CPA or accountant is another task for you to complete. Monthly, quarterly, and annual tax filings and audits are all part of this new game you are playing; shoebox accounting is no longer acceptable. I have seen too many investment opportunities slip away due to lacking or deficient book and record-keeping on the part of a young company. Angel investors want and demand a good, clean set of books and access to your CPA to determine and validate your historical numbers and projections going forward. Creative bill paying is allowed and stock is legal tender with this industry, as with lawyers. Finding the right CPA takes time and proper monitoring. You need a high level of trust here, as both your CPA and lawyer often know more about you and your business than anyone else—even your spouse.

REAL ANGEL INVESTOR COMMENTS AND OBSERVATIONS

1. I am interested in investing in your venture, but your books are a mess!
2. I like you and some members of your team—but where are the older Board members to offer guidance and supervision?

3. I will invest, but first I want to meet with your Board Chair.
4. I am interested in investing in your venture; let me talk to your legal counsel.
5. Who prepared these documents—your teenage son?
6. Get your projections done properly and realistically, and then call me.
7. You are under 30 and need more experienced advice and suggestions. Assemble a board that can offer guidance and oversight.
8. Call me when you have a seasoned Board of Directors.
9. Without proper SEC documents, I would never invest in your venture. Go find a lawyer.

REFLECTIVE QUESTIONS FOR CHAPTER 11

1. Where can I find and pay for a respected Board of Directors?

   _____

   _____

   _____

2. Why do I need a Board of Directors?

   _____

   _____

   _____

3. What can a Board of Advisors offer to me as I grow this business?

   _____

   _____

   _____

4. Lawyer and CPAs are expensive. How can I pay for the best advisors in my space?

   _____

   _____

   _____

5. How and where can I find an attorney and CPA that are a good fit for my business?

_____

_____

_____

12. PAYING CUSTOMERS

YOU ARE NOW INCORPORATED, HAVE FINISHED YOUR BUSINESS PLAN AND tight executive summary, and completed your PowerPoint for presentation at the next Gathering of Angels. You are assembling your management team and members of Boards of Directors and Advisors, and have met several times with your new lawyer—who you found through _____. Your CPA, whom you discovered by _____, is helping with your projections and has assured you he'll be right by your side when the time comes to prepare your tax returns and quarterly filings with the state and IRS. You have made good progress in the last several months, but your cash balance is very low, and you're looking to bring in some Angel Investors to support your dream.

One of the first questions Angel Investors will ask—that you better have the answers to—is: *Who are your customers?* Who will buy your product or service? What are price points and time of payment? Early and even late investors, VCs and most certainly Investment Bankers want to know this information—and rightly so.

All the prior planning and slick presentations in the world will not convince me—or any savvy Angel—that I should invest in your company if you *don't have paying customers yet*. However, with a solid plan and three-year P&L projections from your new CPA, you're in a prime place to begin amassing some. You must take your product or service to market and prove to both yourself and your current and future shareholders that your offering will hold water and fill a real need in the current marketplace.

I have heard the line more than a hundred times, "I know it will sell and will have huge appeal if I can just get your money for sales and distribution." But very few Angel Investors will write you a check if you have no paying customers. Yes, test marketing is critical, and giving the product away to 100-500 customers can be helpful; they can put what you are selling into use and give you good and proper feedback that you can incorporate into your offering. But until you get that product or service *into their hands*, actually collect funds and clear their checks, you can't really attest to the fact that you have true paying customers. They may not all be happy and completely satisfied with your offering but they paid—and the check cleared.

So—who *are* your potential and future customers? Of course, it's ideal to have multiple individuals and groups rather than relying on a single type of customer or client. You want to be able to rely on as many streams of revenue as possible. Landing the big fish is great, but they rarely give you the margins you need for survival. They don't always pay on time and will often drag payments out 30-60-90 days after they sell to one of *their* customers—which means you might well go bankrupt before they pay you. Additionally, "big name" clients and companies will drop you often with no reason when a competitive product is offered at a lower price. The US Government is an example of a huge buyer of good and services—but they pay slowly and, like a big retailer, will string you out on final payment forever.

Instead, it's preferable to have 50-100+ smaller customers who pay for your product or service than one or two big fish who can—and often *do* —jump out of your small boat. Your margins will never be as large—nor will you receive payment as fast—as you will with smaller customers. They will know and appreciate the challenges you're facing, because they've been there, too. When you show them that your offering is what will cure their pain, you'll have made a sale.

Once you've secured these customers, the next step is get honest and valid feedback from them.

REAL ANGEL INVESTOR OBSERVATIONS AND COMMENTS

1. I like you; but have you figured out who your customers are?
2. I have money to invest, but I need to see some solid examples of paying customers.
3. It's foolish to rely solely on a big retailer like Wal-Mart; they could dump you in a minute!
4. Give me some feedback that you've collected from your paying small customers.

5. Give me a list of your customers and details on the input you've received from them, and then I will invest in your company.
6. Have you listened to your paying customers? Have you altered your product or service offering after feedback?
7. When do you get paid? How quickly?
8. I'd advise getting some smaller customers who pay full price rather than waiting 90 + days for a check.

REFLECTIVE QUESTIONS FOR CHAPTER 12

1. Why are paying customers important to you and any potential Investor in your company?

   _____

   _____

   _____

2. Is a smaller customer better or worse that some bigger customers like Walgreens, Kroger, Microsoft, Aetna, or Wal-Mart?

   _____

   _____

   _____

3. Do I have it made if I land Wal-Mart as a customer?

   _____

   _____

   _____

4. What can I learn from early small paying customers?

   _____

   _____

   _____

5. Why do I need early paying customers for my business?

   _____

   _____

   _____

13. INCUBATORS

WHEN YOU HEAR THE TERM *incubator*, YOU LIKELY PICTURE THE HATCH-ing process of chicks. However, it has a very different meaning in this book. In small business incubators around the United States, young entrepreneurs are co-habitating in an environment that allows them to grow faster and stronger. These enterprises' survival rate is much higher than those who operate out of their garage or basement.

Every incubator space and locale is different; over my 40 years of business, I have never seen one that was not unique and distinctive to fit the local community's needs. Incubators in the Silicon Valley or San Francisco are very different that the ones in Atlanta or Boston or Santa Fe. Some incubators are small with only five to ten companies—while others are massive and take up multiple floors.

Incubators have been around since the late 70s and early 80s, the time when technology and the internet arrived on the landscape of business. Some incubators are privately funded and others are for profit; but most are non-profits, often connected with a college or university. Enlightened Small Business Development Centers (or SBDCs, as they're known) will frequently start these incubators to enhance the survival rate of nearby startups. Their hope and assumption is that if a company starts locally and succeeds, it will stay local—as long as capital sources exist to nurture and fuel the growing business's capital needs.

Both private and university sponsored incubators began to appear in Atlanta in the mid-80s. Some, like the Advanced Technology Development Center or ATDC, have managed to weather the storms of multiple recessions and still exist today as a major part of their local business community. I have been involved in starting several incubators—one non-profit in Santa Fe in the early 90s, and one for profit in downtown Santa Fe in 2000. The latter had four companies as tenants and offered space, high speed internet connections, and access to capital sources through the Gathering of Angles and a side by side VC fund.

You might wonder—why do I need an incubator at all? What can they offer that I cannot get by operating out of my garage? Incubators—and accelerators, which we'll discuss in a bit—offer joint space and resources, shared conference facilities, break rooms, multiple levels of talent, service providers like legal, accounting, web design, SEO, and social media support. While you can get some of these services as a solo entrepreneur working from your basement office, an incubator has it all in one place. Garage life can get lonely, and cabin fever is not a disease you want to catch while concentrating on your start-up. Having other companies that are at the same stage as you nearby can be comforting and supportive. Being able to share ideas, theories, and crazy dreams with others in a supportive environment is huge for a young company just getting started.

Finding good and helpful legal and accounting support is also close at hand in an incubator. Many offer weekly classes on topics such as QuickBooks, patents, and capital attraction over brown bag lunches and after work seminars. Retired senior executives frequently give their time, talents, and contacts by referral to those companies inside incubators. For example, Atlanta's ATDC has a deep roster of retired executive level talent to assist the tenants as they grow and mature; I've lectured there myself on several occasions. Such environments provide a great depth of support and guidance as a company matures. They regularly provide classes on business plan and executive summary development and further refinement at no charge, in addition to holding social events and parties to build a sense of community, camaraderie, strength and support—all the things that are missing from your garage. You can locate a well-run and properly financed incubator in most major metro cities.

You can expect guidance, direction, encouragement and even capital leads if not actual capital investment from an incubator's management and senior staff. Seed capital is the most difficult of all portions of the funding process. As you know by now, it's daunting enough to pull money from your 401k plan or savings and then tap friends and family for the next round. But nothing is as intimidating as going before a group of total strangers and asking for a capital investment in your young pre-revenue business.

Incubators can and should help you navigate this process and prepare you for this next step on the capital trail. They can help you construct your 12-20 slide PowerPoint presentation, tighten your executive summary, give guidance on required securities documents, and assist you with legal and accounting needs. But always remember—like your Boards, while the staff is there to support, they're not there to run your business for you. That is a job for you and your management team to complete. Until you outgrow the space, spending 9-12 months in a well-run incubator should help you prosper and grow to maturity. Very few baby chicks would survive alone if left to fend for themselves in the wild. Only inside a hatchery or incubator can they grow and remain safe from the elements—and from the wolves, coyotes, and other wild animals that would like a young chick for dinner. Your situation is not all that different; finding and joining financially sound incubator is a smart decision.

Given the advent of online education and learning, it likely won't be long before online or virtual incubators pop up. This will give more small-town entrepreneurs access to guidance, direction, and maybe even capital. We are studying this as a potential offering from the Gathering of Angels website later this year—specifically, offering incubator services from the cloud on a subscription basis for six, nine, or twelve month periods. CEOs of startups that aren't located near major cities don't always have a nearby incubator. But with high speed internet access, they'll be able to access a virtual incubator. Simply by opening up your laptop, you are in business—and getting the guidance, sage advice, and mentoring you need to succeed.

REAL LIFE ANGEL FEEDBACK AND OBSERVATIONS

1. You need help with your business plan and ideas. Have you looked into a local incubator? That could be the ticket.
2. Life in the garage is lonely. You need folks to bounce your ideas off of.
3. I started in an incubator when I launched my business, and it made all the difference in the world for me.
4. All Incubators are different, so shopping around can be a smart idea.
5. I am a retired senior executive and I enjoy teaching and mentoring at my local incubator.

6. The best place to find senior talent for your Boards is in an incubator.

7. The classes and comradeship in the incubator is amazing.

REFLECTIVE QUESTIONS FOR CHAPTER 13

1. What are the benefits of time spent in an incubator?

   _____

   _____

   _____

2. Money is tight; can I afford life in an incubator for 3-6 months?

   _____

   _____

   _____

3. Are all incubators alike?

   _____

   _____

   _____

4. Where can I find out about a close incubator to me?

   _____

   _____

   _____

14. CORPORATE LOCATION

BACK WHEN THE ENTREPRENEURIAL BUG FIRST BIT YOU AND YOU DECIDED to start a new data management and encryption company, you were enjoying the good life in the small town of Gravel Switch, Kentucky. You'd graduated from MIT several years before and met a lot of wonderful and very bright classmates, but you decided to return home to rural Kentucky to be closer to your parents. After all, they're the ones who put you through college and are now supporting your dreams and latest schemes with this new company. They have invested over 100K in your new venture—so you try to see them several times per week.

However, you experienced a few problems when first starting out. For one thing, the high speed Internet connections in Gravel Switch are only fair to poor, whereas you had blazing fast connections and streaming data back in college. Additionally, ice and snow make moving around country roads in your home town challenging during the winter. Your high school sweetheart has now become your wife and a new baby is on the way. You had enjoyed working in the family insurance agency that your grandfather started, where your Dad is now, and you are his able Senior Vice President at 25 years old. But you were getting antsy and realized you wanted a new venture—and it didn't take long to see that Gravel Switch was likely not the best corporate location if you plan to grow the new business.

Even with the internet connectivity problems, small town USA presents other challenges to ensuring that your new venture prospers. Life is slower and more pastoral, yes; but many things needed for your success are missing. With a population of only 33,000 good folks, it's often difficult to find good legal and accounting advice closer than 150 miles away. There is an incubator on the edge of town but its only inhabitants are young chickens and not other entrepreneurs. The average age in Gravel Switch is 64.5 and the retirement home and assisted living facility have a long waiting list for their 40 beds. Clearly, this isn't the place to get your business going.

Your wife had suggested that moving 150 miles away to Louisville might be a good idea; while you could still see your parents regularly, you'd be closer to the action. Your research has shown that other data management companies are now moving to the Alpharetta area—north of Atlanta—because of the big pipe, optic cable, and more consistent cell phone coverage, more talent, infrastructure, and greater sources of capital. Your new business plan predicts that your current staff of three will need to grow to 200 in three years; those folks neither live in Gravel Switch nor will they be willing to move there. The town's two decent restaurants and three fast food places, along with the "fair" public school ranking, aren't exactly encouraging young families with children to flock there. While your grandfather gave you his home before he passed away, it's not nearly modern enough, nor will it have enough room for your growing family. The stage is set for a move and renting an office close to the action. You decide that the time is right to start looking for a new residence and a new location for your corporate headquarters. Now is the time to move to Alpharetta, get wired in, join the Chamber, start looking for new staff, and move ahead with growing your business.

You began paying rent for space in your new corporate location—but then came across an abandoned data center vacated by Home Depot. This is perfect for you, as it has an adjacent 3000 square feet of office space configured to your current needs and some future growth. In your new location, you will find many more talented prospects for your upcoming staffing needs, thanks to nearby college and university satellite campuses. Better schools and infrastructure will allow you to attract and retain the talent your business plan calls for over the course of the next several years. You are a smart guy—but you can't do it all alone. You know that you must surround yourself with the smarter talent you'll only find in larger metropolitan centers.

Your business plan also calls for you to develop a Board of Directors and Board of Advisors. Fortunately, it looks like you'll encounter at least some of these folks in and around the Atlanta area. The population of six million people in the nearby metro area is flush with executive talent and recently retired folks. They have put down roots there, and they aren't moving. Major centers like Atlanta also have top level legal and accounting firms and spin offs that can help you grow your business. You will be pleased to find supportive banks, 15-16 Venture Capital firms, and 2-3 different Angel groups, all in the Atlanta area. Several of the money center banks do have investment banking operations and many boutique investment bankers are most helpful to growing companies and their capital finance needs.

You decided to relocate for the opportunities that Alpharetta, Georgia afforded, and the pool of talented potential employees and advisors it offered. You found a fast-paced life style, inexpensive housing, excellent schools, and many options for higher education that simply aren't available in the small town where you grew up.

Some entrepreneurs may need to consider moving for the access to capital. Small town and even remote resort locations rarely match the capital available in metro areas. The Atlanta, Dallas, Boston, New York, Chicago, Los Angeles, and San Francisco areas are hubs of talent, C-suite executives who can be helpful with skills and referrals—and often with access to capital. A move from a smaller town to one of these metro areas will almost certainly increase your business's chances of survival and ultimate success. Of course, you will also need to be close to your customers. Remaining in touch with them will show them you care about their patronage—and shorten the supply chain.

REAL LIFE ANGEL INVESTOR OBSERVATIONS AND COMMENTS

1. Why in the world is your headquarters in this tiny town no one's ever heard of?
2. Excellent public and private schools and higher education are important to me—and small towns just cannot offer that. I pass on your offer to join your Management Team.
3. I will join your Board—but I'm not moving to Small Town, USA.
4. Come to the big city for quality employees who you can train and retain for years to come.
5. Your business is located too far away for me to be helpful.
6. I have the money to invest in you but you need to move closer to me so I can watch your progress and correct your mistakes when I see them.

REFLECTIVE QUESTIONS FOR CHAPTER 14

1. Why should I leave small town paradise and move to a big city?

_____

_____

_____

2. What are advantages of big metro area over small town for business growth?

_____

_____

_____

3. Where can I find the talent I need to grow my new business?

_____

_____

_____

4. Is seed and early capital available in big metro centers vs small towns?

_____

_____

_____

15. WEBSITE, SEO AND SOCIAL MEDIA

WITH YOUR NEW BUSINESS PLAN IN HAND, YOUR MANAGEMENT TEAM formed, and your relocation to an urban metro center, you are ready for your corporate website, URL and imbedded SEO-Search Engine Optimization. Marketing 101 would suggest that you need to be known by customers, clients, staff, and sources of capital to grow your business. In today's digital world, a new venture without a professional website is dead in the water. One of the first requests coming your way from Angel Investors will be: "Give me your URL and web address. I want to know more about you—and I will be prepared to discuss your business and find out more about your management team and advisors when we meet."

When I first started the Gathering of Angels in Santa Fe in 1996, I offered the concept and idea to the Albuquerque based non-profit that held once a year investment seminars. However, they declined my offer, saying it was too much work monthly. Once I received their rejection, I decided to move ahead on my own. I knew that I needed a website to market my angel forum event. I knew back then, as I do today, that young companies looking for capital will do a web search for an Angel Investor or seed capital. When they do, you need to be there on the web and in a prominent position on the major search engines.

Because web designers are never inexpensive, I decided to do this myself on INC.com. This magazine and its website offer a template that anyone, even someone with very little technical know-how, can use to fill in the blanks, save, and post to the world-wide web in under 30 minutes. *And*, it was cheap. Soon enough, my site was up and alive—and I was in business.

It worked for a while; but as I looked around at other professionally prepared site, I soon realized that my amateurish efforts reflected on my new venture—and that I needed more skilled assistance and direction.

One of the clients for whom we'd raised capital was called Voyager Communications. They created and hosted my new GOA site for the next five years, providing monthly updates and posting fundings success stories. This professional effort brought me many new clients, and young firms from all over the USA began to inquire about presenting at my Santa Fe Gathering of Angels. The GOA website was working wonders, and the SEO component had me on page one when a young start-up venture went to the web searching for an Angel Investor.

I have worked with four different webmasters over the past eighteen years. My most recent web designer, based in Big Canoe, Georgia, is called Interactive Search Marketing. They've done an exceptional job with a newly designed and themed site and have added more functionality than previous efforts. SEO, or search engine optimization, has been imbedded in the site and on the home page and my rankings on Google, Yahoo, and Bing have returned. The number of daily hits I've received have increased substantially in the months since the new site was launched. Because the algorithms that search engines employ change regularly, designers must stay abreast to ensure high rankings and remain on the first few pages of key words. I use my 5-6 key words every day to check that the Gathering of Angels site is ranked highly, that all links are functioning, and dates for upcoming meetings are accurate and complete.

I cannot emphasize enough how important a crisp, relevant, and professionally done website is to your success. Customers, clients, potential investors, potential staffing hires, advisors, mentors all will look at your website today as the window to the world for your new venture. Take the time and spend the money with your new web designer to get it right. Review your site every day to confirm full functionality and accuracy, and to post new information, blogs, and new press articles for even higher ranking on the major search engines.

Social Media is another marketing tool for your new business. A presence and participation on Facebook, LinkedIn, and Twitter can encourage new clients, customers, and prospective new hires to connect with you and keep them posted about your new venture. I have gotten new presenters from all of these social media outlets. Though I initially resisted having this much exposure, I eventually realized that the more folks know about what I do and how I serve the needs of young start-up companies, the better. Most basic accounts are complimentary; more advance offerings are monthly subscription based and can be helpful and instructive for more detailed information gathering. Local classes on perfecting the use and implementation of Social Media can be helpful for those who find these new platforms challenging and confusing—or even just those who want to get the most out of the experience.

REAL LIFE ANGEL INVESTOR OBSERVATIONS AND COMMENTS

1. Give me your URL and I will check you out.
2. Where is your website?
3. I did a search on your company, and you are not on Google's top 10 pages.
4. You are all over the web—I like what you are doing.
5. I see you have a website, but no presence on Facebook or LinkedIn. Why not?

REFLECTIVE QUESTIONS FOR CHAPTER 15

1. Why do I need a website and URL for my new business?

    _____
    _____
    _____

2. What is SEO and why is it important?

    _____
    _____
    _____

3. How do I set up SEO for my business?

    _____
    _____
    _____

4. I am 60 years old and a first time Entrepreneur. How can I get help doing Social Media marketing?

    _____
    _____
    _____

5. Where do I find a good Web Designer?

_____

_____

_____

6. What can I do to keep my website on page one on Google?

_____

_____

_____

16. LESSONS LEARNED AND SUMMARY

AFTER 18 YEARS OF LEADING THE GATHERING OF ANGELS, WATCHING 2,000+ presenters come through the process, and matching over 380+ capital fundings, I've certainly seen my share of trends and footprints emerge. Every GOA night is different; every presentation has its unique characteristics and subtle nuances. Some presenters are confident, polished, and very well prepared; others are nervous, having never taken the stage asking for money. All presenters today are graded and receive marks from each attending Angel Investor at my meetings. These GOA Presenter Evaluation sheets are completed as a requirement of attendance and reviewed by GOA staff. We then give these to the presenters after his/her 20 minute presentation and two to five minute long Q&A session.

These provide invaluable feedback and critique of the presentation style, delivery, and content. We let each participant know how their presentation went and how they handled their Q&A sessions. Attendees will rank the presenter based on presentation quality, understanding the business model, financials, management team, and exit strategy. They then circle investment interest and how they would like to be followed-up with. If the angel has no investment interest, there is a spot to note this—and no follow-up or calls from a presenter are allowed nor encouraged. If there is investment interest and the Angels circle an investment amount, the presenters review this; then set up follow-up meetings and calls. We encourage immediate follow-up; the quicker an entrepreneur is to accelerate the requisite due diligence period and consummate the investment, the better it is for everyone involved.

Who gets money from Angel Investors and who does not is an art form in the highest degree. Preparation, practice, and tenacious follow-up of investment interest is quite simplistic but accurate. Delayed and prolonged follow-up is rarely productive and always frustrating. All presenters at my Gathering of Angels events pay a fee to present their company with no percent of capital raised. They don't come to GOA for networking, backslapping, and card swapping; they're there to raise seed and early stage capital for their venture. As such, networking folks and service providers are not allowed to attend GOA meetings; if we discover that they're in attendance, we ask them to leave and never return. Time is precious at these meetings; for an entrepreneur to spend time with a non-check writer is counter-productive and non-remunerative. Though they will need such professionals later down the road, a lawyer, CPA, or web designer's presence at the initial GOA events is unnecessary and a waste of time.

Preparation with a strong business plan, a very tight one page Executive summary, a well-rehearsed 12-20 slide PowerPoint, and concise answers to potential questions from the audience is the key to successful capital rising. One also has to be confident and knowledgeable about his/her service or product offering, its potential in the marketplace, and have high passion and enthusiasm about his or her company. Poor, ineffective communicators rarely get capital funding. The 20 minutes afforded by the GOA business model goes very fast, and there are never rewards for long winded presentations with no awareness of when the bell is going to go off.

95% of all of the industries and services reviewed and considered are allowed to present once we've vetted the offering and pitch and presenters have paid the necessary fee. We do not have a specialty, sweet spot, or industry preference; I have found capital for software, hardware, medical device, restaurants, B&Bs, products, soft drinks, wine and beer offerings, and energy drinks.

When you and your management team decide that the time has come to raise seed and early stage capital—after you've exhausted your savings and other sources of capital, and fully tapped your support of your new venture—then it's the proper time to make contact with individual Angels and Angel Clubs and Forums. Raising this critical capital requires that the CEO or Chairman make a direct commitment; it's not something that you can delegate to a marketing or finance person, broker, or advisor. By committing this level of talent, proper time in preparation and precious resources, you'll be ready to present your product or service offering for proper funding from Angel Investors.

I wish you great success in your journey toward funding of your new venture. I trust that the advice I've provided in this book will be an invaluable resource to you and a constant reference as you move forward to growing and prospering your business venture. Godspeed.

Tarby Bryant
Chairman and CEO
Sweetwater Capital Corporation / The Gathering of Angels
10145 Big Canoe
Jasper GA 30143
706-579-1080, 404-606-2193(cell)